THE SOPHIOLOGY MAN
THE WORK OF VLADIMIR SOLOV'ËV

The Sophiology Man

The Work of Vladimir Solov'ëv

Aidan Nichols, OP

Gracewing

First published in England in 2020
by
Gracewing
2 Southern Avenue
Leominster
Herefordshire HR6 0QF
United Kingdom
www.gracewing.co.uk

No part of this publication may be reproduced, stored in a retrieval system, or transmitted in any form or by any means, electronic, mechanical, photocopying, recording or otherwise, without the written permission of the publisher.

The rights of the Trustees of the English Province of the Order of Preachers to be identified as the author of this work have been asserted in accordance with the Copyright, Designs and Patents Act 1988.

© 2020 The English Province of the Order of Preachers

ISBN 978 085244 873 1

The publishers have no responsibility for the persistence or accuracy of URLs for websites referred to in this publication, and do not guarantee that any content on such websites is, or will remain, accurate or appropriate.

Typeset by Word and Page, Chester, UK

Cover design by Bernardita Peña Hurtado

CONTENTS

Preface   vii

1. The Making of a Sophiological Philosopher   1
2. The Theosophy Project   39
3. The Theocratic Writings   69
4. A New Start and the Final Coming   93
5. Sophiology's Nemesis?   115

Conclusion   149

Bibliography   157

PREFACE

This book is an introduction to the personality and thought of the founder of Russian sophiology, the philosophy and theology of 'wisdom', Vladimir Sergeevich Solov'ëv (Владимир Сергеевич Соловьёв).[1] Some years ago, I wrote a 'Primer' for the study of Solov'ëv's principal disciple, Father Sergeĭ Bulgakov, whose dogmatics—displayed in two trilogies, one 'Lesser' and the other 'Great'—is the most substantial attempt at theological construction in the Russian Orthodoxy of the modern period—or, indeed, ever, for that matter.[2] Although by the time Bulgakov came to write his mature works he had become his own man, and was no longer so dependent on Solov'ëv's philosophical speculations, he cannot really be understood without a grasp of the thought processes of his eccentric yet highly gifted predecessor.

Furthermore, by common accord, Solov'ëv remains the single most important philosopher Russia has as yet produced. There has been an explosion of interest in, and writing about, him in the country since the ending of Soviet period constraints in the later 1980s. And since the closing years of the twentieth century there has likewise been an unexpected outbreak of 'philo-sophiology' in the West, and this, while it principally concerns Bulgakov's theology, can hardly avoid entirely Solov'ëv's philosophical endeavours.[3]

All in all, then, it was high time for me to come to terms more fully with this nineteenth-century figure, opposed by the rationalist, materialist and socialist thinkers of late tsarist Russia and severely criticized by a number of Orthodox commentators, Father Georges Florovsky prominent among them (I outline his views in my last chapter), in the century that followed.

When honing his opinions on ethics, epistemology and ontology Solov'ëv wrote lucidly—if, for some critics, too sweepingly, not pausing sufficiently to consider objections to his demolitions of the arguments of others. He did not, though, leave behind a fully coherent body of reflection on the 'Lady' Wisdom celebrated in such sapiential books of the Old Testament as Proverbs and the Wisdom of Solomon—the 'Sophia' that gives 'sophiology' its name. His sources here were a mixture of Christian and Jewish, both exoteric (from the public realm of the official Scriptures and the 'monuments' of Tradition) and esoteric (from marginal Christian writers and the Jewish Kabbalah), together with some highly personal experiences he claimed as his own. I have done my best to render his sophianic doctrine intelligible to the reader. Its aims are apparent: first, to avoid both pantheism and a Godless account of finite reality, and secondly, to do justice to the receptivity inscribed in both the divine world and the created world in which we live.

In this book there will also be found an account of Solov'ëv as an early 'ecumenist', concerned with the reunion of the Orthodox and Catholic Churches—and indeed with the reunion of Christians all round. His 'scheme' would hardly fit the circumstances of Christianity today. It depended on the survival of the tsardom, a Christian monarchy to which he ascribed a leadership role for world society in a commonwealth of nations. It also assumed that the claims made for the Roman bishop at the First Council of the Vatican (1869–70), namely, infallibility and universal jurisdiction, are unproblematic as they stand. The discussion of a 'universally primatial' see taking place in the current dialogue between the Eastern Orthodox and Roman Catholic Churches, and the difficulties for the internal coherence of Church doctrine—and appropriate freedom of speech in the Catholic episcopate—caused by initiatives taken in the pontificate of Pope Francis, suggest that the opposite is the case.

After an early 'theosophical' stage (nothing to do with the celebrated or notorious Madame Blavatsky) where Solov'ëv's interests were concentrated on an 'integral' or 'holistic' grasp of *the true*, and a middle 'theocratic' period when his mind was concentrated on how to achieve, for Christendom and global society, the common *good*, Solov'ëv moved into a late 'theurgical' phase dominated by such themes as nature, art and love (though the good and the true were not forgotten). These topics could perhaps be summed up as anterooms of the third of the great 'transcendentals' of Christian Scholasticism: namely, *the beautiful*. This too receives some attention here. In particular, I attempt a comparison with the 'romantic theology' of the English critic, poet and dramatist Charles Williams.

But even within its modest limits this introduction would not be a proper account of its subject if it failed to mention Solov'ëv's last offering to the world. At the end of his life, his many-sided intellectual, ecclesiastical, political, moral, and aesthetic enterprise morphed into the belief that only divine intervention, in the form of the Parousia of Christ, will ever resolve the myopia, lethargy, folly and other evils of *homo sapiens* on this planet. Among those evils he identified one attempted 'final solution'—a globalist utopia organized without reference to the incarnate God. The *Legend* [or '*Short Story*'] *of the Antichrist* was Solov'ëv's last message. It is perhaps his most pertinent word to people today. On 26 February 1900, having read the text to a packed audience in St Petersburg, he added his own interpretation in the following words:

> Such is the impending and inevitable dénouement of world history. We shall not see it, but events of the not-too-distant future throw their prophetic shadow, and in our lifetimes more clearly and undeniably than ever do counterfeit good, fraudulent truth and fake beauty rise before our eyes. All the elements of the great deception are already before us, and our immediate descendants will see how all these things shall interweave and come together in one living and individual phenomenon, in Christ turned inside out, the Antichrist. The most profound meaning of world history is the fact that in this final historical phenomenon of the principle of evil there shall be such a great deal of good. It is required that the prince of this world be allowed to show himself toward the end from the best angle, to become freely adorned in every semblance of good. Only when he has exhausted everything that can be finally unmasked, he openly appears in his own form of evil, lies and monstrosity—only then can he in truth be condemned and of necessity perish.[4]

Works cited without author are Solov'ëv's own.

NOTES

1. Russian is transliterated following, essentially, the British Standard, but well-known names such as Tolstoy or those of writers such as Florovsky who published primarily under a simplified form of their name are given in their more familiar forms; absolute consistency is impossible to achieve.
2. Aidan Nichols, OP, *Wisdom from Above. A Primer in the Theology of Father Sergei Bulgakov* (Leominster: Gracewing, 2005).
3. Antoine Arjakovsky, 'The Sophiology of Father Sergii Bulgakov and Contemporary Western Theology', *Saint Vladimir's Theology Quarterly*, 49.1–2 (2005), pp. 219–35.
4. Cited in Oliver Smith, *Vladimir Soloviev and the Spiritualization of Matter* (Brighton, MA: Academic Studies Press, 2011), pp. 168–9.

✣ 1 ✣

THE MAKING OF
A SOPHIOLOGICAL PHILOSOPHER

Vladimir Sergeevich Solov'ëv was born in Moscow in 1853, the second son of a distinguished professor of Russian history who went on to become rector of the University of Moscow. Sergeï Mikhailovich Solov'ëv's studious habits, love of Russia yet rejection of an over-narrow patriotism, as well as openness to some at least of the criticisms of Orthodoxy emanating from the Latin West, would re-emerge in novel forms in the outlook of his son. Their relations, however, appear to have been formal rather than close. Solov'ëv's paternal grandfather Mikhail Vasil'evich Solov'ëv was an Orthodox priest, remembered with fondness though he died when Vladimir was only eight. He may have been the model for the 'Elder John' in *The Legend of the Antichrist*.[1] Solov'ëv's last major philosophical treatise, *The Justification of the Good*, dating from 1897, would be dedicated to father and paternal grandfather alike.[2] The forebears of his mother Poliksena Vladimirovna, *née* Romanova, a family of the service nobility—those ennobled for services to the State, in this case military—came from 'Little Russia', i.e. the Ukraine. She would outlive her husband by thirty years, and her son by nine. Solov'ëv, much of whose correspondence is addressed to her, took from his mother his dark colouring and a temperamental inclination to 'premonitions',[3] but not the indifference to domestic arrangements which rendered him in later life a nomad living between hotels and the houses of friends, his books and other few possessions scattered among them. Monies he earned or otherwise received he commonly gave away. Solov'ëv was certainly no stranger to the almsgiving, fasting and prayer he took to be the three pillars of Christian practice.

In the autobiographically revealing late poem 'Three Encounters' (dating from 1898), he remembered a childhood love at the age of nine, which may or may not be an echo of Dante's first sight of Beatrice according to the *Vita nuova*.[4] At any rate, it looks like the beginning of his life-long fascination with 'the Eternal Feminine', at once a literary motif in European culture, best known from its use by Goethe, and a link with an eclectic mix of religious traditions for which 'Sophia'—Wisdom—was either a dimension of uncreated divine being or a primary form of created being or both of these together. A mystical experience in church would overshadow this precociously early experience of romance in what he took to be a first actual encounter with his 'eternal companion', the Lady Wisdom, as 'Three Encounters' bears witness.[5] The iconostasis was open and there came towards him from the sanctuary a lady:

> Holding in your hand a flower from unearthly lands,
> You stood with a smile of rays of light,
> Nodded to me and disappeared into the mist.[6]

Perhaps unsurprisingly, the Swiss theologian Hans Urs von Balthasar surmised that this (and the other two 'meetings', yet to come) might be an experience of the Blessed Virgin Mary.[7] For the Orthodox priest-theologian Sergeĭ Bulgakov and the literary critic Konstantin Mochulskiĭ, an early biographer of Solov'ëv's, the reports were affected by unconscious association with icons or mosaics of the Mother of God.[8] In none of the three encounters described in the poem of that name does Solov'ëv call the lady 'Sophia'. Usually he simply speaks of her as 'you', though he can also write 'queen', 'eternal friend', or (more alarmingly) 'goddess'. In his poetry Solov'ëv could address with the words 'earth-mistress' the cosmic entity or alleged entity he called the 'world soul'. The latter was a feature of ancient Platonist and (especially) Stoic cosmology revived in the *Naturphilosophie* of some German thinkers in the early nineteenth century. Here Friedrich Wilhelm Joseph Schelling is the name to reckon with. For Schelling, nature is unconscious spirit, and spirit is nature become self-aware. The world soul was a relatively constant element in Solov'ëv's cosmology, too. In poems where the title 'earth-mistress' appears he was in effect apostrophizing nature as an organized whole. Aware that the similarity of the two images, the 'queen' and the 'mistress', could cause confusion, he tried to clarify it in the preface to the third edition of his poetry, published in the year of his death, 1900.

There was indeed a connexion of sorts between the mistress and the queen. As the American Solov'ëv scholar Samuel D. Cioran comments, 'What Solov'ev celebrates in any feminine principle other than Sophia, what he celebrates in the World Soul or nature or earthly beauty, is not that earthly material nature itself, but rather the reflections, echoes and premonitions of the divine Sophia, who is invested there in potential form'.[9] Solov'ëv warned against the possibility of deceptive likenesses of Sophia.[10] By the end of his life he was more and more convinced that the 'world soul', the supposed instrument of Wisdom in guiding the world process, had in fact been seduced by evil. Increasingly chaotic, its condition was rendering possible the reign of Antichrist, understood as a seemingly progressive but really false and even diabolic version of Christianity. In his last writing *Three Conversations* (1899), Antichrist's empire, and the persecution of the small remaining minority of faithful Christians and Jews, is the cue for the Parousia, the Second Coming. By this juncture, then, 'his original vision of a *radiant* and *serene* apocalypse—with Sophia at its head—was to be replaced with a darker vision of impending cataclysm before the final proclamation of God's kingdom on earth could be uttered'.[11] That implied, of course, a continuing 'hope for the union of heaven and earth', albeit in altered form.[12]

After his early seminal experience in church, it might seem surprising that only a few years later, at the age of fourteen, he abandoned not only Orthodoxy but all religion for the cause of scientific materialism. (Critical biography might find here a reason for supposing at least the first of the sophianic 'encounters' to be poetic licence.) From 1869 to 1871 he was enrolled as a student in the Faculty of Sciences (the Physical-Mathematical faculty) of Moscow University. Though he made a special study of plant morphology and comparative anatomy, by his own account it was the philosophical aspect, or philosophical implications, of the natural sciences which most interested him.[13] He discovered the seventeenth-century Dutch rationalist philosopher Baruch Spinoza, whom initially he took to be a materialist—until he realized how untenable a materialist interpretation of Spinozist thought actually is.[14] Spinoza's contemporaries had indeed considered him an atheist (he did, after all, reject the ideas of creation and of a personal Providence). But at the turn of the eighteenth and nineteenth centuries he was rediscovered as, in the words of the Romantic poet who wrote under the nom-de-plume Novalis, a 'God-inebriated man'. Was Spinoza's God absorbed into the world, as atheists thought? Or was Spinoza's world absorbed into God, as theists (or pantheists) believed? Whichever way, Spinoza's definition of divinity (*Deus sive Natura*, 'God or Nature') as *causa sui et causa omnium* ('the cause of itself and the cause of everything else') enthused the young Solov'ëv, awakening his delight in systematic philosophical thought and giving him a first glimpse of what might be called his own controlling intuition.

That intuition was summed up by his mid-twentieth-century biographer Maxime Herman as a conviction of the 'spiritual uni-totality of the world'.[15] The Russian-Jewish philosopher Semën Frank, an admirer, claimed that 'the intuition of this unity determines the whole of Solovyov's world-conception'.[16] Sergeï Mikhailovich Solov'ëv, the writer's nephew, in his 1923 biography, the manuscript of which was smuggled out of the Soviet Union in the 1970s, agreed.[17] The 'spiritual uni-totality of the world' is also key to some more recent interest in Solov'ëv. In the early twenty-first century the claim is often made that if, in a 'post-theistic' age, we 'are to have a God, it should take some pan(en)theistic form': words of the Louvain-based Irish philosopher William Desmond.[18] If uni-totality be indeed Solov'ëv's root philosophical concept it is not surprising that Spinoza's influence gave way in due course to that of German Idealism, which opened a door to a wider realm of relevant possibilities. The key Solov'ëvan term behind 'uni-totality', *vseedinstvo*, 'all-unity', looks suspiciously like a Russian translation of the German word *Alleinheit*.

In the first place, this shift of allegiance to the Idealists meant discipleship of Arthur Schopenhauer the pessimism of whose chief work, *The World as Will and Representation*, lay heavy on Solov'ëv till the cloud was penetrated, if not entirely dispelled, by another feminine encounter. This was the episode, recorded in his memoir 'At the Dawn of a Mist-shrouded Youth', when an unknown woman saved him from falling to his death between two carriages of a railway train in motion.[19] The railway accident, when the twenty year old Solov'ëv briefly lost consciousness and, on recovery, saw in a transfigured light the young woman who had saved him, seems to have played a major role in changing his mind-set from a radical pessimism to a confidence that life has some meaning and in all likelihood a plenitude of it.[20]

The personal correspondence of this young man suggests a slow recovery of Christian faith. Transferring from the faculty of Sciences to that of Letters (or 'Liberal Arts', and more especially the department of History and Philology), he acquired a decent familiarity with the great philosophers—even if it would never be expressed with the kind of scholarly apparatus expected of historians of philosophy in the twenty-first-century academy. Plato and the Neo-Platonists ranked high in his eyes. Not less eminent in his estimation were the German Idealist philosophers Friedrich Wilhelm Joseph Schelling, in his later period, and the now largely forgotten figure of Eduard von Hartmann who, like Schelling, sought to reconcile some form of Idealism and natural science. Thanks to auditing courses at Moscow's Ecclesiastical Academy, situated outside the city at the shrine of the monastic founder and national hero St Sergius of Radonezh—an unusual undertaking for a university student with no aspirations to priesthood, and one that temporarily cut him off physically from his peers—he also picked up the elements of theology. It is reasonable to suppose that this was when he came across the biblical theme of the Wisdom of God. That theme gave him an at least superficially plausible scriptural justification for the Sophia-mystique found not least in 'Three Encounters'.[21] A foundation was laid for subsequent exploration of how post-biblical Judaism had treated the Wisdom-figure. Those explorations exemplified the maxim of the twentieth-century philosopher Paul Ricœur, 'The symbol gives rise to thought'.[22] 'Jewish traditions of commentary on the meaning of divine Wisdom made use of the Platonic theory of ideas, the Aristotelian understanding of God as self-thinking thought, and the Stoic cosmology of *pneuma-logos*. Jewish commentators came to conceive of divine Wisdom as "the ultimate and total object of God's thought on creation and the history of salvation, but without ever immersing God into the world or divinizing the world".[23]

The last sentence of that citation pinpoints the neuralgic issue in Solov'ëv's thinking for his co-religionists—and indeed for all Christians who are orthodox (with a lower case 'o') in their view of the God-world relationship. Before his late period—the time of the celebrated or notorious 'Legend of the Antichrist'—has Solov'ëv 'immersed' God in the world? Is this a reduced God who, like the world itself, is simply part of a wider whole? If so, what has happened to the transcendence of God, the radical difference from the world that enables God to be intimately present to it? There is a problem with the notion that the 'whole' is more than just God. It is part and parcel of the concept of God that there can be nothing 'more' than God, nothing greater than him. See the celebrated description in St Anselm's *Proslogion*: God is 'that than which nothing greater can be conceived'.[24] *Vseedinstvo*, the 'all-unity', cannot trump God.

But might we at least say that the world is *continuous with* God, in which case we could legitimately use the language of 'emanation' to describe their relation. That idiom is not altogether unknown in patristic and mediaeval usage (including by St Thomas[25]). Alternatively, as suggested by the more frequently encountered term 'creation', sanctioned as it is by the Creeds of East and West, are God and the world *dis*continuous?[26] The absolute Origin of the world is surely other than the world. And yet one could venture to ask, in Desmond's words, 'Is there a between that holds open the space of qualitative difference of God and creation, which enables creation to be as other while yet allowing communication between the two?'[27] (The notion of 'between' [*metaxy*] is Desmond's favoured tool in metaphysics, hence his coining of the neologism, 'metaxological'.) A survey of Solov'ëv's development and writing such as the present study should help the reader to judge.

In his early years at the University of Moscow Solov'ëv's letters indicate the influence of the Slavophile philosopher Ivan Kireevsky, who died when Solov'ëv was three.[28] For Kireevsky, keen to locate some unique—actual or potential—Russian contribution to the culture of Christendom overall (that is one possible meaning of the term 'Slavophile'), the Christian faith contains within it a higher rationality, a rationality which is not, as yet, despite the valiant efforts of the ancient Christian writers, fully disengaged. Kireevsky judged 'patristic philosophy' to be in this context desirable yet also 'insufficient; ... it must enrich its living truths by the thousand year experience of reason [i.e. post-patristic philosophy] and adapt the results of Western science to Christian belief, alive in Eastern Orthodoxy'.[29] In Kireevsky's view, Russia, which had both a deeply rooted Orthodox faith and a philosophically instructed elite, was a country well placed to accomplish this task, laying the foundations for a new and improved quintessentially Christian intellectual life.[30] Solov'ëv would eventually rally to this account of Russian uniqueness. He was already convinced that the faith had not yet found its sufficient expression. His correspondence shows him reading the 'Greek and Latin theologians of the ancient Church' which he deemed to be something 'necessary for the complete understanding of Christianity'.[31] It is a mistake to suppose that his own religious philosophy was worked out in complete ignorance of the Fathers, though followers of the 'neo-patristic school' in twentieth-century Orthodoxy, who are allergic to his religious philosophy, sometimes give this impression. He came to regard the seventh-century Church Father Maximus the Confessor as the greatest philosophical mind of ancient Christianity—with the exception of Origen. But Solov'ëv's mature expression of hope for human salvation was much more Maximian than it was Origenist.[32] Kireevsky too had profited by the revival of the study of the Fathers in late tsarist Russia, in his case via not so much the theological academies as the monasteries.³³ The affinity between the overall aims of Kireevsky and Solov'ëv is striking. As Marina Kostalevsky has observed, 'Both writers consider one of the causes for the emergence of rationalist philosophy to have been the gap between theoretical thought and religious faith, which disrupted the harmonious integrality of the human being. They are both dissatisfied with the achievements of Western philosophy and express the need to create, in Solov'ëv's words, 'the *universal synthesis* of science, philosophy and Religion', or as Kireevskii put it, 'the integral consciousness of reason imbued with faith'.³⁴

Solov'ëv was now reading widely in the texts of other religions, notably for his 1873 essay 'The mythological process in antique paganism', which also shows the influence on him of Schelling and Alexeï Khomyakov. Khomyakov, a Slavophile collaborator of Kireevsky and the leading lay theologian of Nicholas I's reign, was an obvious choice of guide.³⁵ But why Schelling? Actually, the early Slavophiles had already experienced his attraction. The English Jesuit historian of philosophy Frederick Copleston explains. What the Slavophile thinkers

> wanted was, not so much adoption of Schelling's philosophy as such, as the development of a specifically Russian line of philosophical thought. It was the late phase of Schelling's philosophizing which came to attract them, when Schelling was criticizing Hegelianism as a 'negative philosophy', as a logical deduction of abstract concepts allegedly divorced from concrete existing reality. In their view [i.e. that of Russian students of philosophy] Schelling showed an awareness of historical reality in its varied organic development, an awareness which could serve as a point of departure for the emergence of a recognizably Russian philosophical tradition, in harmony with the Orthodox religious spirit.³⁶

Obviously enough, salvation history and, subsequently, Church history, are vital to Orthodoxy: they deal with the gradually prepared coming of the God-man and then his ongoing work through the community—the Church—he founded on earth. Schelling's thinking was, however, hospitable to metaphysical speculations strange by the standard of patristic or Scholastic benchmarks, Eastern and Western. He had learned from, as well as influenced the eclectic Bavarian Catholic thinker Franz Xaver von Baader, whose use of Eckhart and Böhme produced a heady cocktail of mysticism and philosophy.[37] So far as Solov'ëv was concerned, the fact that Schelling had written a treatise on the philosophy of mythology would obviously have attracted the attention of a young philosopher wishing to investigate the 'mythological process'.

Yet in this essay Solov'ëv was not an uncritical admirer of either figure. He disagreed with Khomiakov's 'take' on ancient paganism. For Solov'ëv, a religion of the 'free spirit'—ascribed by Khomiakov to the Iranians—existed in antiquity only in Israel. And Solov'ëv departed from Schelling on the topic of pagan myth. Schelling found human culture's myth-making activity 'objective' in the strong sense that behind that activity lay 'theogonic forces'—in other words, the divine was itself in process of coming to be, a process reflected in the development of human myths. Solov'ëv was enough of an orthodox (lower-case 'o') Christian to reject any notion of a developmental 'becoming' of God, which is implied, or indeed stated, in Schelling's *Potenzenlehre* (which is not to say that the mature Solov'ëv did not have his own account of how the 'other', whether uncreated, as in the Word and Spirit, or created, as in the world-idea, could be 'posited' in God).[38] For him, the objectivity in question consisted in the fact that humankind could only 'conceive the divinity according to its [the divinity's] material manifestations', i.e. the way the divine perfections are expressed in the creation, the world around us.[39]

Solov'ëv's own attempt to show how a (postulated) primitive monotheism turned into a (quite undeniable) polytheism in cultural history was suggestive for his future thinking. To be encountered by human beings the divine has to manifest itself.

> He who manifests himself is the same supreme God. But beside him appears the material cause of the manifestation, primordial nature, which receives his formative action and

which, in determining [that action] passively, produces a world of new forms. As a receiving and bearing principle, it is a feminine force; primitive man, ignorant of abstract notions, personified it under the traits of a feminine divinity, the first goddess, the universal mother (*mater—materia*), by consequence of which the supreme God appears as an exclusively masculine divinity, as the universal Father.[40]

Here we have the first appearance of a feminine divine principle of some kind (not yet, however, termed 'Sophia') in his philosophical works. From this initial rupture in the fabric of monotheism—this was how Solov'ëv's thinking ran as an historian of religion—the development of polytheism could readily be inferred.

In this essay Solov'ëv was influenced by the characteristic Idealist approach to history at large. History can have no meaning unless, taken overall, it is a teleologically conceived ('goal-directed') development. He continued to think of history in this way until the sudden shift to apocalyptic thinking in the final years of his life. That was a consequence of the non-appearance of historical changes he had hoped to see unfolding in his lifetime.

Solov'ëv's brilliance, already signalled in this early essay, indicated a likely university post as docent (assistant professor) in philosophy though the actual appointment was owed more immediately to his first book-length study *The Crisis of Western Philosophy: Against the Positivists*, a master's thesis dating from the year of his election, 1874.[41] On his analysis in that work, rationalism and empiricism are simply two versions of a purely formal, rather than concretely real, approach to existence.

Rationalism's remote origin Solov'ëv placed in the work of the ninth-century Irish divine John Scotus Eriugena (an unusual departure-point, maybe taken from Kireevsky).[42] As Solov'ëv saw things, the rational tradition developed in two major phases. First, with Descartes, Spinoza and Leibniz, 'an independently existing reality corresponds perfectly to the innate general ideas we have of it.'[43] Then with Kant, Fichte, the early Schelling and Hegel, for whom cognitive activity depends on *a priori* categories, true being comes to be located, rather, in the supreme forms of human thought. Hegel is indeed the acme of this process, since with Hegel, 'that which is, is a concept'.[44] It was, to Solov'ëv's mind, unsurprising that reaction to this climactic version of speculative rationalism took the wildly contrarian form of vulgar materialism.

Empiricism moves on a different historical trajectory—beginning with Bacon and moving via Locke and Hume (and, contrapuntally, Berkeley) to an apogee in John Stuart Mill. Here true being is reducible to states of human consciousness, and thus to empirical experience. Neither of these claims struck Solov'ëv as remotely plausible. These philosophies only answer the question *how* man knows. They hardly touch on the question *of what* it is he knows in knowing what is real. 'Both the rationalist and the empiricist directions of modern philosophy concluded that what truly is, is mental or "abstract"... Epistemology as an abstract, philosophical discipline annihilates itself, for both directions ultimately affirm that cognition, cognition of what truly is, is unattainable'.[45]

Yet when un-diverted by unilateral philosophies, it is proper to human beings to seek the true nature of reality as it exists in and of itself. That is so not least because on the nature of the real there turn the criteria of morals: viz., the norms for what people should do, for how they should act. In more or less the opening words of *The Crisis of Western Philosophy* Solov'ëv explains his motivation in writing. 'This book is based on the conviction that philosophy in the sense of abstract, *exclusively* theoretical cognition has ended its development and passed irretrievably into the world of the past'.[46]

The statement, though sweeping, was not meant to be dismissive. Earlier philosophies such as, precisely, rationalism and empiricism produced genuine, if limited, advances in understanding which can contribute to a overall resolution of the question of truth, a resolution the philosophies in question are by and of themselves unable to attain. Schopenhauer saw this, but his efforts to create an 'integral inner synthesis' foundered on an obsession with the subjective representation of yet another abstraction—a never-to-be-satisfied will or desire.[47] For Schopenhauer, the stimulus to metaphysical reflection is not wonderment at existence but confrontation with death when will and desire terminate, and this naturally inclined him to pessimism. Schopenhauer's disciple Hartmann had also learned from Leibniz for whom the world is a system of enclosed units, 'monads', presupposing as these must an Absolute—an infinite, all-encompassing reality—by means of which particular beings, though self-enclosed, can nonetheless exist in real relations with the cosmos as a whole. Solov'ëv 're-read' the (nonetheless, Schopenhauerian) Hartmann through an optimistic looking-glass. Hartmann had proposed, in the spirit of Schopenhauer, the desirability of a cosmic annihilation in time, juxtaposing this supposed desideratum with the affirmation of an Absolute outside time. Solov'ëv re-wrote Hartmann as looking forward to the annihilation not of existents but of *separateness*. Specifically, the inter-relation of all things in their shared relation to the Absolute would be realized by a process of evolutionary development, itself tending to 'the suppression of the exclusive self-affirmation of isolated beings' by virtue of their responsiveness to the 'universality of the absolute spirit'.[48] Thus doctored, Hartmann's ontology could be hailed as the acme of Western philosophical development so far—and the supreme indicator of Western philosophy's ripeness for a happy marriage with the Christian faith.

Contemplating the general scene of 'modern' Western philosophy and its epistemic discontents, Solov'ëv himself now made a 'gigantic leap' into speculative metaphysics.[49] The 'logical and empirical elements of cognition' are surely 'united or synthesized prior to and presupposed by consciousness', which, for him, 'confirms ... that "in our cognition we are concerned with what exists independently, which also posits the possibility of metaphysics"'.[50] That demonstrates there must be 'an essential identity between metaphysical essence and the knower, i.e., our spirit', the human spirit functioning here as a 'particular manifestation' of a universal spirit (the initial letter in this second instance should probably be capitalized) the character of which is to be 'all-one'—to possess that all-important *vseedinstvo*.[51]

Leap or not, that is where Solov'ëv's metaphysics indeed begins, as his introductory lecture as a newly fledged 'docent' of the University of Moscow demonstrated.[52] Solov'ëv's robustly metaphysical thinking was by this date unfashionable among the intelligentsia. The émigré scholar Marc Raeff, professor of Russian studies at Columbia University in New York, drew a sharp distinction between the 'thirst for genuine spiritual fulfillment and free creativity' among the intellectuals of the 1830s to 1840s—the so-called 'marvelous decade'—and what subsequently transpired in the 1860s and 1870s. Raeff wrote,

> It is the extremism, dogmatic stubbornness, uncouthness, as well as aggressiveness of the men of the 1860s that were the source of the loss of the spiritual gains made by the 'marvelous decade'. By contrasting themselves to the older generation of the elite, by rejecting all idealism and spirituality, by their exclusive scientism—especially on the biological model—and by their intellectual intolerance, the men of the 1860s and their followers exercised a regime of unofficial censorship and intimidation that forced much of Russian spiritual and aesthetic life into a penumbra zone of public neglect.

And Raeff went on to name Solov'ëv as one of the few writers who

> succeeded in weakening their tyrannical hold. It is, however [Raeff regretted to report], this heritage of the 1860s that continued to dominate the socially and politically engaged members of the elite. The socialist parties, especially the Bolsheviks, and the anti-cultural populism that also originated in the 1870s ... preserved these attitudes and helped them to their triumph in 1917. It was a victory of the secular utopian mode of thought in its crassest form and with the most destructive consequences for Russian as well as for European culture.[53]

As things turned out, Solov'ëv's academic tenure in Moscow was rather brief. He would resign his post in 1877, probably owing to internal politics. (Seemingly, he would have liked to roll back some of the liberal university reforms of the 1860s.) But it was long enough for him to become seriously interested in Gnosticism, a curious topic for a philosopher—though Schelling had taken more than passing notice of it, and among the Renaissance neo-Gnostics Jakob Boehme had long been influential in Russia.[54] A doctorate was a sine qua non if he was ever to hold a professorial chair. The topic in question, complex, amorphous and hard to untangle, was suited to the scale of a doctoral dissertation. In the academic system of the tsarist era, foreign travel for the purposes of research was a normal university practice. What was not normal was Solov'ëv's decision to repair not to one of the German Universities then favoured by Russian scholars but to London, whither he duly went with an official mandate to study Gnostic, Indian and Western mediaeval philosophical texts in the British Museum. The premier (if unsympathetic) present-day student of Solov'ëv's intellectual development, Thomas Nemeth, remarks how he 'may have harboured ulterior motives for wishing to go abroad for a period of study.'[55] The Sorbonne professor of Russian history Dmitri Strémooukhoff, in his study of Solov'ëv's 'messianic work', says outright he was chiefly looking for material on 'The Lady'. In Strémooukhoff's view: Solov'ëv, schooled by the sapiential books and Jewish esotericism, had at last allowed himself to believe in 'her' as Wisdom—whereas previously he had felt he was forbidden so to do by the Old Testament prophets, who were clearly hostile to any notion of some sort of female 'consort' for the God of Israel.[56] Yet not until the *Lectures on Godmanhood* (completed in their written form in 1881) would he give a theoretical account of what he took Wisdom to be, appealing there not only to the Old Testament sapiential books but also to the letters of St Paul.[57]

In London he got to know the co-discoverer of biological evolution, Alfred Russell Wallace, a figure with a lasting interest in extra-sensory perception and associated mediumistic phenomena. Solov'ëv was fascinated. But his interest in spiritualism was soon replaced by a more enduring concern with the Jewish Kabbalah, accessed, it seems, via *Kabbalah denudata*, the work of a German scholar, Christian Knorr von Rosenroth, who between 1677 and 1684 glossed with interpretations of his own the three volumes of the principal kabbalist source-book, the Zohar, which itself dates from the late thirteenth century.[58]

The Making of a Sophiological Philosopher

In esoteric Judaism, affected as this was by the Gnosticism of the first Christian centuries, the Infinite manifests Itself by putting out 'emanations' (in Hebrew, *sephiroth*), ten in all. These emanations are what make possible the worlds of finite being. On Strémooukhoff's analysis, Solov'ëv discovered in the British Museum library the kabbalistic distinction between the second *sephirah* 'Hokmah' or Wisdom (the name is masculine in gender) and the tenth *sephirah*, 'Malkuth' or Kingdom (the name here is feminine). 'Malkuth' appears in kabbalistic lore as a second Wisdom. By contrast to 'Hokmah', 'Malkuth' is the 'Wisdom of the End'.[59] The notion that Wisdom is not only primordial, at the beginning of creation, but eschatological, at the consummation of creation, and that between these two there is a significant developmental narrative, would be an idea of the greatest importance for Solov'ëv's thinking.

He seems to have read the Kabbalah through Schelling-tinted glasses. He concluded that 'the real and mystical connexion of all that exists qua incarnation of a unique and absolute content is the departure point and fundamental principle of the Kabbalah: a conscious and systematic anthropomorphism is its fulfilment'.[60] The 'real and mystical connexion of all that exists', is of course *Alleinheit*, alias *vseedinstvo*. But the combination of theism, cosmology and anthropocentricity indicated in the rest of the sentence quoted was common to Jews and Christians alike. The unwieldy but convenient term 'theoanthropocosmism' has come into use for a set of emphases which, one can say, is crucial for the Russian sophiologists. One goes to God through a cosmos which has its own intended centre in man, the priest of the world.[61]

In the Reading Room of the British Museum he had another vision of the Lady Wisdom. He was led to believe she was inviting him to go to Egypt where a further experience of 'her' transpired in the desert. What exactly he was looking for in Egypt remains unclear. He may have been aware that the Old Testament Wisdom literature had Egyptian models, and perhaps took Isis to be the ancient Egyptian version of Sophia. There might be an indication in an odd prayer he wrote out. His nephew believed it to be his own composition whereas Bulgakov, his principal theological disciple, thought he had merely copied it from some source. It is a rather sinister or at least occult text (hence, no doubt, Bulgakov's unwillingness to ascribe it to Solov'ëv), inasmuch as it appeals not only to the Trinity but to 'gods and demons and all the living', asking them to capture the 'pure dove of Zion', before addressing Sophia directly and asking her to 'appear to our eyes under a visible form, adding "incarnate yourself in us and in the world by reestablishing the plenitude of the ages" so that God may be all in all'.[62] Whatever he was looking for in Egypt, and despite the confirmatory apparition of Lady Wisdom, he seems to have been disappointed in his quest, returning after four months via Sorrento, Naples and Paris. He had told his mother he was working on a 'mystical-theosophic-philosophic-theurgic-political treatise',[63] and the string of adjectives does in fact faithfully anticipate the contents and manner of the bulk of his ensuing writings.

The eclecticism of subject-matter is well represented in a set of four French-language manuscripts of this period, collectively entitled—significantly enough—'Sophia'. (The manuscript was impounded by the Soviet secret police in 1931 from the apartment of Solov'ëv's nephew and biographer Sergeï, and eventually made its way, along with the biography,[64] to the Russian State Archives for Literature and Arts. Illicitly copied, both texts were brought to France in 1972.) Two of the manuscripts are simply monologues ('La Sophia') but the others ('Sophie') take the form of dialogues between a philosopher and a mystically minded feminine figure, 'Wisdom'. As might be expected, they combine philosophical analysis with mystical speculation. If we can assume that the Sophia-character represents Solov'ëv's own views, the opening dialogue suggests a notion of the fulfillment of Christian teaching which goes far beyond Kireevsky's—and not in a direction Orthodox belief could support. The philosopher-character enquires whether the 'universal religion' described by Wisdom is still 'the religion of Christ and the apostles'. Is it 'Christianity in its perfection, or does it have another principle?'[65] Wisdom's initial reply is reassuring for the Orthodox. 'The universal religion is the fruit of the great tree whose roots are formed by primitive Christianity and trunk by the religion of the

Middle Ages. Catholicism and modern Protestantism are dried up and fruitless branches it is time to lop.'[66] But then she adds, 'The true universal religion ... is the real and spontaneous synthesis of all religions, which robs them of nothing positive and then gives them what they do not possess.'[67] But possibly the treatise is an aberration, later recognized as such by its author. Thomas Nemeth, who certainly has no interest in serving a Church-standpoint, comments: 'Clearly written while Solov'ëv was, for whatever reason, standing on the brink of a mental crisis, "Sophia" is quite arguably more a psychological testament to his state of mind at the time than it is a piece of philosophy or even theosophy.'[68] And Nemeth adds two further considerations. 'We should not forget that Solov'ëv did not refer to this work later in his life, and it was preserved only owing to the careful vigilance of his nephew', while 'in his later years, Solov'ëv distanced himself both emotionally and intellectually from his early interests in the occult and spiritualism.'[69]

This is perhaps the point at which to mention some slightly disturbing reports which raise the question, Was Solov'ëv entirely sane? According to his friend the lay theologian Prince Evgeny Trubetskoy, who contributed to the first book-length study of Solov'ëv, in 1911, during bouts of illness the philosopher was prey to hallucinations. A Russian researcher at the British Museum, writing the previous year, reported how in all important decisions Solov'ëv claimed to enjoy direction from a deceased Frenchwoman of the sixteenth or seventeenth centuries. He is known to have practiced 'automatic' or mediumistic writing, which sometimes took the form of erotic letters signed 'S' (presumably for Sophia). Quite a lot of strange material of this kind appears to have been destroyed by Solov'ëv's brother Mikhail after Vladimir's death. Against this, one might cite a frequent sign of sanctity in both the Eastern and the Western traditions. We hear that 'animals loved him and [more unusually] flocks of birds besieged his hotel room.'[70] The Russian existentialist philosopher Nikolaï Berdyaev who, like Bulgakov, went into exile after the Revolution of 1917, spoke in this connexion of a 'day-time' or highly rational Solov'ëv and a 'night-time', or sometimes bizarrely mystical Solov'ëv.[71] The night-time

Solov'ëv found more generally acceptable expression in his poetry than in his religious experimentalism. Here, then, was 'a theoretical philosopher of the highest order who was subject to prophetic dreams and diabolic visitations, who looked on philosophical truth with the eyes of an enthralled visionary'.[72] However else Solov'ëv may be characterized, 'ordinary' will never be the right word to describe him.

In any case, the day-time and night-time figures cannot be too sharply contrasted since the poetry and the philosophy were themselves not 'divorced'.[73] In Solov'ëv's view, the poet evokes in images the higher meaning of existence as expressed by the philosopher in rational concepts.[74] In his late-period essays on aesthetics ('Beauty in Nature', 1889; 'The Overall Meaning of Art', 1890), just as beauty in nature 'by "transilluminating" and spiritualizing matter ... helps to raise up the fallen World Soul and to introduce an element of the divine into reality', so likewise beauty in art acts as 'a theurgic force capable of transforming and "transilluminating" the human world'.[75] Solov'ëv sees the artist as called to offer premonitions of the eternal beauty that is at once another world from this and yet is drawing closer to our world in time. That would render art, then, a prefiguration of the consummated condition of all things. So far as the Lady Sophia and other variants on the Eternal Feminine are concerned, Samuel Cioran offers a useful comment. 'In keeping with the philosophical views of the poet, the only constant and fixed star is Sophia, whereas the extra-divine feminine principle in nature or womanhood is "free" to accept God's Wisdom and strive for union with Him, or to assert itself contrary to the divine principle of total-unity'.[76] The question remains, of course, what *is* 'Sophia' anyway?

Coming home to Russia, Solov'ëv abandoned his Muscovite university post, being named instead to membership of the Academic Committee of the Ministry of National Education at St Petersburg. He also met Sofia Petrovna Khitrova, the separated wife of a diplomat, sensing around her a sophianic halo well suited to her name. He remained for a good part of his life mesmerized by the image of this woman, his 'Madonna of the Steppes'. Not that this atrophied his capacity for intellectual articulation. In fact he was now seeking to organize his philosophical reflections as in the 1877 *Philosophical Principles of Integral Knowledge*; the 1877–81 lectures which became *Lectures on Godmanhood*, and the 1880 *Critique of Detached Principles*, his doctoral thesis.

The 'integral knowledge' that figures in the title of the first of these publications, is a recognizably Slavophile motif. Like the Slavophiles, Solov'ëv believed in a distinctive philosophical role for the Russian nation. In 1876, the year before he published his philosophical synthesis, he had read a paper at the Muscovite 'Society for the Lovers of Russian Literature'. Perhaps under the influence of the Pan-Slav revival occasioned by Turkish atrocities in Bulgaria, Solov'ëv allotted to the Slavs in general and Russia in particular a task of philosophical leadership for the future. 'Three Forces' (this was the paper in question[77]) sees the Islamic world as gripped by a despotic concept of God inimical to personal development, and Western Europe dominated by a political individualism destructive of human solidarity and a positivistic scientism incapable of addressing, much less answering, the great questions of human life. That cannot, surely, be the final tally of civilizational experience. There must be some social setting, either actual or potential, where science, philosophy and theology can be held together in a vision of human life that explicitly includes relation with the divine. The choice cannot just be between 'the inhuman God', on the one hand, and 'the godless human individual' on the other. Fortunately for the world there is another country where 'East and West meet and transcendd their spiritual division in a higher religious principle'—and this principle is God-manhood, *bogochelevechestvo*, 'divine humanity', or 'the humanity of God'.[78] In Thomas Nemeth's paraphrase of Solov'ëv's conclusion in this essay:

> Since all *other* nations that have or are playing an influential role in world history are under the predominant influence of one of the first forces, only Russia can serve as the mediator between the rest of the world and the divine world ... Although we cannot know when the disclosure of Russia's

mission will occur, all indications are that it lies in the not too distant future, even though that nation may not be aware of its epochal task.[79]

The Philosophical Principles of Integral Knowledge was originally serialized in the St Petersburg *Zhurnal ministerstva narodnogo prosveshcheniya*, though publication was broken off, and the work left incomplete.[80] Its important introduction furnishes Solov'ëv's view of the wider historical process at this time. In Maxime Herman's précis, he 'takes the world to be an organism in course of development. This development takes place in three phases: to the initial unity succeeds a differentiation among themselves of the elements that constitute the world and which a final synthesis again unites.'[81] Considered historically, the world of pagan antiquity, an intricately united religious whole, is succeeded, from the dawn of Christianity onwards, by a series of disassociations—of religious society from civil society, of civil society from economic society, until at last only individuals remain, and give rise to such ideologies as Positivism, Socialism, and Utilitarianism. This unsatisfactory condition of modern Western culture must itself give way, yielding place to a fresh unity where, however, the now differentiated elements are integrated without being simply subsumed. Thus a new richness will ensue in a *tsel'nost'*, 'integrality' or 'wholeness', where human and divine are united. Strémooukhoff commented:

> The notion of integral life which synthesizes human functions in an organic whole, represents from one side the continuation and development of Slavophile integralism ... But from the other side it is more still: the integral life is also the life of a universal organism, it is conceived as the union of the divine and the human. Thus it is the notion of the integral life which allows Soloviev to make the synthesis of his personal mystical intuitions with the ideas inherited from Slavophilism.[82]

Mystical, empirical and rational must be synthesized, awaiting a larger synthesis of theology, philosophy and the sciences at large. Entirely in the manner of *The Crisis of Western Philosophy*, where Solov'ëv found rationalism and empiricism wanting as approaches to reality, he presents empiricism and idealism as, in their ultimate conclusions, self-refuting. In Nemeth's words, 'what truly exists is not empirically cognized, nor is it cognized by pure thought'.[83] What truly exists, inaccessible to rationalism and empiricism, announces itself in its reality in the external world and in its ideality to human thought. The principle of the real is, accordingly, both super-cosmic and super-human: to conceive it suitably is appropriately termed 'mysticism', though this way of intuitive encounter needs completion from those contributions of reason and experience which rationalism/idealism and empiricism/naturalism have wrongly taken as self-sufficient and all-important. At this point in Solov'ëv's treatise it is not entirely clear, however, whether 'absolute reality' or 'the truth' is actually God—or simply the ontological structure of the world.[84]

In any case, only by integral knowledge, integrating within itself mysticism, empiricism and rationalism, is it possible to have knowledge of reality's foundation. As *The Philosophical Principles of Integral Knowledge* continues to unfold, it becomes plain that Solov'ëv's target is not just a general ontology, a study of being as foundation for both material phenomena and thought. He aims beyond this at an account of the *principle* of being—namely, God himself. His concern now is not with 'absolute reality' in the sense, purely, of what, speaking generally, truly exists, but in the further and more pregnant sense of the *ultimate source* of the truly existing. This, then, is the 'Absolute', suitably capitalized in English prose since it takes its place among the many synonyms Solov'ëv used for God.

Solov'ëv proposes that the foundation of reality (in its twofold sense—both general ontology and Ultimate Principle), can be explored via three disciplines. And these are: logic, which considers the Absolute in its primordial undifferentiated condition; metaphysics, which studies the Absolute insofar as it gives rise to the finite world, and ethics inasmuch as the Infinite unites Itself to the finite in a differentiated unity.

Most important for his religious philosophy in *The Philosophical Principles of Integral Knowledge* is the way Solov'ëv's 'organic logic' ventures an account of an Absolute, which, in manifesting itself, differentiates itself as Trinity.

> If the absolute were to remain only itself, excluding its other, then this other would be its negation, and as a consequence it itself would no longer be absolute ... the not-absolute would be outside of it as its negation or boundary, and as a consequence it [the Absolute] would be limited, exclusive, and not free ... Thus when we say that the absolute first principle by its very definition constitutes a unity of itself and its negation, we are repeating, only in a more abstract form, the words of the great apostle: God is love.[85]

That argument, taken alone, favours not so much a Trinity as a Bi-unity, God and his Logos, God and a Second in God: the Father's eternally generated Word. But then Solov'ëv takes a further step.

> Every kind of self-manifestation contains from the perspective of that which is being manifested, three necessary, general aspects: (1) that which is being manifested in itself or of itself, in which the manifestation consists of a concealed, or potential, state; (2) the manifestation as such, i.e. the affirmation of itself in an other or on an other, the discovery, definition, or expression of what is manifested, its Word, or Logos; and (3) the return of that which is being manifested into itself, or the self-discovery of that which is being manifested in manifestation.[86]

The last is Solov'ëv's philosophical version of the eternal Father's further self-revelation in a divine Third, the Holy Spirit, making God, indeed, triune—the BlessedTrinity.

Here Solov'ëv's project corresponded, at any rate in part, to that attempted a generation earlier in the Catholic West by the Austrian priest-philosopher Anton Günther. Neither Pope Pius IX nor the First Council of the Vatican (1869–70) had favoured Günther's rational demonstration of the Trinity. The grounds for dislike were the same as those exhibited by Solov'ëv's friend and critic Prince Evgeny Trubetskoy when he enquired: 'If the highest truths of the divine life can be deduced a priori and known by the natural forces of pure reason, then, one may ask, what is the role of [specifically Christian] faith?'[87] Solov'ëv might have answered, as in his later encyclopaedia article on the twelfth-century Latin theologian Hugh of St Victor: 'The recognition in these three manners that the three self-acting subjects are persons—namely, the Father, the Son and the Holy Spirit—surpasses reason but does not contradict it'.[88] In other respects, Solov'ëv's theological rationalism in *The Philosophical Principles of Integral Knowledge* exceeds that of Günther—a 'semi-rationalist' for whom demonstration of the truth of Trinitarianism can be offered only a posteriori: that is, subsequent to its historic disclosure in positive revelation.[89] Still, the attempt to find *rationes necessariae* that throw light on the intelligibility of Christian revelation had a long pedigree, stretching back in matters of Trinitarian theology to Marius Victorinus and Augustine (at whose hands, however, the 'necessary reasons'—a phrase associated with St Anselm—might be better described as illuminating analogies[90]).

The departure point of the logic, absolute Being considered before its manifestation, receives from Solov'ëv not the biblical or patristic name 'Father', but the kabbalistic name of *En-Soph* ('The Infinite'), while the determinations of the Absolute which it sets forth in the course of its manifestation constitute the contents of the mind of the Logos—which, in the Gospel of St John and the Greek Fathers ranks as an alternative name for the Father's Son. The contents of that mind are composed of organically inter-related ideas of whatever is other than God. There exists in God, then, and more specifically in the Logos of God, the possibility of a *further* divine self-manifestation, which this time will eventuate in a *world*. That world will in due course enter the minds of human beings who, alone of all creation, will be able to perceive it not only in its internal relations but in its relations to the Absolute as well—in other words, to see things in the 'all-unity'.

Expressed in kabbalistic terms, the Logos can thus be identified with a 'primordial humanity' eternally existent in God. The Logos constitutes everlastingly the centre of the all-unity of God's world, a world which, 'before' time, is only as yet divinely imagined. The task of centring creation—holding it together by understanding, by activity—is a role the human race is to take up as its defining mission in time, in history. The unity of the intelligible world which eternally coheres in the Logos is to be rendered incarnate by human efforts in the temporal creation.

The Greek Fathers, like the Western mediaevals, would have agreed with Solov'ëv in locating the 'intelligible world' in the Logos of God, the second Trinitarian Person.[91] Balthasar compares the early Alexandrian theologian Origen's concept here with the more nuanced scheme employed by the seventh-century Byzantine doctor St Maximus. 'By conceiving of the Logos—as Origen had done—both as the second Person in God and as the locus of the divine ideas, Maximus is led to conceive the world as an unfolding of the unitary divine Idea and so comes close to the idealist notion of an "economic" return of all things in the world to their idea in God.'[92] Balthasar cites a text from the *Ambigua*, Maximus's commentary on difficult passages in his patristic predecessors:

> Who would not recognize the many *logoi* [the intelligible principles of things] as the one Logos, who through all the process of drawing all things upward to himself, remains unconfusedly himself, as the essential and individually distinctive divine Logos of God the Father, the origin and cause of all things, 'in whom all things were made, things in heaven and things in earth, the invisible and the visible, thrones, principalities and powers: all things were made from him and for his sake'.

—an internal citation of Paul's letter to the Colossians 1:16.[93] For Maximus, the divine ideas can also be described as divine decisions, acts of the divine will, and thus include the divine 'plan' for the fulfillment of created things which takes place through the Incarnation and the Paschal Mystery. 'It is very significant', wrote Balthasar, 'that Maximus represents the Incarnation of the Logos and the whole historical course of the world's salvation as both a primeval idea of God and as the underlying structure of his overall plan for the world.'⁹⁴ This historical—and ultimately eschatological—'take' on divine creation will also be of key importance for Solov'ëv's teleological—goal-directed—understanding of creation by the divine Word.

The question obviously arises, then, of the relation between God's Logos and his Wisdom. Not till the *Lectures on Godmanhood* will much be offered by way of clarification of this issue, but it may help the reader if I anticipate a little here. In the *Lectures* we shall learn that in the all-unity constituted by divine agency two distinct unities are comprised. One unity is productive, and this belongs to the Logos. The other unity is produced, and it belongs to the Idea (capitalized 'I'), the totality of the creative thoughts in the divine mind *when these are conceived as distinct from God*, for they are thoughts of what is 'other' than God—precisely in that created world which will enter into being with the advent of time. To the Idea, so understood, Solov'ëv gives the further name of Wisdom—Sophia.⁹⁵

Insofar as Wisdom is not simply the content of God's creative mind but can also be considered as distinguished from God—vis-à-vis God or over against God, a reality altogether distinct from him—'she' has as 'her' proper instrument the 'world soul', the *anima mundi* of the Latin Platonists of the Middle Ages. The soul-of-the-world is not, as we might think, a way of describing how the cosmos subsists as an inter-connected living totality. Rather, Solov'ëv conceives the soul-of-the-world as an active subject, a real agent—as soon appears when Solov'ëv's begins to speak of the soul's fall.

Wisdom as divine Idea, the archetypal world in God, is immune to all deficiency. It cannot 'fall' inasmuch as it is God himself. But Wisdom inhering in the soul-of-the-world, Wisdom as a creaturely manifestation of God, capable of being not only distinguished from God but seen over against him, is a very different kettle of fish. It *can* 'fall' and, as things turn out, it *does*—like the Sophia of those ancient Jewish-Christian heretics the Gnostics. 'If the Gnostic Sophia fell from the pleroma for having wanted to know the Father, the soul of the world for Solov'ëv falls for having wanted to possess the whole by herself and not insomuch as it is conferred by

God.'[96] The result is rupture of the world's unity, the transmutation of its elements, and their self-affirmation in isolation (shades of Hartmann's metaphysics), all of which amounts to the entry of evil into the world. The notion that Sophia can fall, not a claim ever encountered in Scripture or the Fathers, would be minimized if not quite eliminated by Bulgakov, for understandable reasons.[97] It was a weapon in the hands of Orthodox opponents of sophiology who, in the later 1920s and 1930s, mounted a campaign against him with considerable, though not universal, episcopal support.

For the 'fallen Sophia' was incontrovertibly a Gnostic survival.[98] The best-known and probably the most coherent version of Gnosticism, Valentinian Gnosis, undoubtedly held an attraction for Solov'ëv, though parallels in handling the Sophia concept should not be exaggerated.[99] His articles on 'Gnosticism' and 'Valentinus and the Valentinians' in the 'Brokgaus-Efron' encyclopaedia, a monument of scholarship in late tsarist Russia, seek to give the Gnostic impulse a philosophical rationale. They are admiring of Valentinus's genius. But they also echo the critique of Gnosticism mounted by the second-century theologian St Irenaeus[100]—a feature of the articles that, granted Solov'ëv's independence of temper, cannot entirely be ascribed to the sobering effects of ecclesiastical censorship. Most likely, Solov'ëv thought he could sanitize, if not Christianize, the notion of the fallen Sophia, just as Schelling had tried to do in his 1809 treatise *Philosophical Inquiries into the Nature of Human Freedom*. 'There Schelling offered a theory of the pretemporal fall or self-alienation of Sophia-Humanity from the divine ground of being and interpreted the cosmo-historical process as the drama of alienated Sophia's struggle to be reunited with her heavenly ground.'[101] In Solov'ëv's case (as I read it) the fall of Sophia is not a pre-condition, or accompaniment, of the creation. Rather is it a recurrent possibility in creation's history—above all, by way of human deficiencies though also increasing them. If one accepts the notion of a world soul (not that the present writer does), it may well imply some kind of *perichoresis*—some degree of mutual affecting—as between rational individual souls and their cosmic counterpart.

The Making of a Sophiological Philosopher

It follows from Solov'ëv's account of the origin of creaturely Sophia that created Wisdom can be made good ('redeemed') only by entering into ever new conjunctions—moments or phases of union—with the Logos: a dramatic cosmic proceeding which unfolds through a series of stages with, cumulatively, happy results. Solov'ëv takes his overall understanding of the phases of that process from Schelling, with the history of nature leading to man, and the history of man, entailing as it does a progressive revelation of God, leading to the Incarnation at Bethlehem of Judaea at the start of the Common Era. Unlike Schelling, however, Solov'ëv understands the Incarnation in an orthodox manner, in the light of the Christology of the Council of Chalcedon, the 451 Council which defined Jesus Christ as one person living in two natures, divine and human, two natures that are inseparable yet unconfused.

What Solov'ëv would bequeath Bulgakov—and thus the attempt to make sophiology the foundation for Orthodox dogmatics—was a pair of problems. Firstly, and this for many was the more damaging difficulty, Solov'ëv's rich prose-style, combining rigour with lyricism, threatened to leave it unclear just where the boundary between the Uncreated and the created lay. Yet without a clear concept of that boundary one can hardly begin to write or teach Christian theology: a datum of patristic thought since Origen. Solov'ëv's most persistent Orthodox critic, Georges Florovsky, was adamant in his defence of the crucial importance of the 'intuition of creaturehood' for Christian theology, and yet, surprisingly, could—sometimes, if not always—treat Solov'ëv's account of the God-world relation as generally deficient yet unobjectionable on this particular score. Bulgakov was able to clarify the matter by a more sustained insistence that 'Wisdom' denotes both an uncreated and a created reality: there are two inter-related yet distinct Wisdoms, one divine, the other creaturely. As he wrote,

> The Divine world and the creaturely world are correlated with one another as the eternal Sophia and the creaturely Sophia. Being identical in their foundation, the Divine world and the creaturely world are different in their mode of being. The

former is pre-eternally existent in God, whereas the latter, as having arisen 'out of nothing', is a becoming world, although Sophia is the foundation and the entelechy for it too.[102]

In effect Bulgakov did for Solov'ëv's speculations about Wisdom what in the fourth century St Athanasius the Great had done for the Wisdom language of pre-Nicene Christianity whose ambiguities had been exploited by the Arians. There is a 'distinction (in unity) between Wisdom in its uncreated and created manifestations'.[103]

The second problem bequeathed by Solov'ëv was that of relating the divine Sophia to the Holy Trinity. Not till Bulgakov do we find a sophiologist writing of Wisdom in fully Trinitarian terms: setting out to relate the Father's Wisdom to both the Logos and the Holy Spirit. As Bulgakov writes in *The Wisdom of God*, the English-language summary of his sophiology: 'The Holy Trinity possesses her as its triune subject, as it exists in three different Hypostases; and in its tri-unity has her as its own Ousia [nature] which in its revelation is the divine Sophia',[104] and again, 'The Son and the Holy Spirit together, inseparable and unconfused, realize the self-revelation of the Father in his nature'.[105] In brief: the Wisdom of God is, qua uncreated, the content of the divine nature in its creativity; qua created, it is that content insofar as it can be replicated in creation; it is so replicated by what Irenaeus calls the two 'hands' of the Father, namely, the Son and the Spirit, in their conjoined work in creation, salvation and the consummation of the world.

Bulgakov's theology, though it is, for historic Christianity, the most valuable outcome of Solov'ëv's life and work, constitutes for the historian just one particular deployment of Solov'ëv's heritage. A full overview of that heritage is only possible once the gamut of a lifetime's writing has been surveyed. But Cioran's compendious summary may help to orient the reader's as the first chapter of the present study draws to its close. 'Just as Sophia represents the produced oneness in the divine sphere and the potential unifying of the extra-divine or chaos with the divine, so also will she symbolize the possibility of an actually produced oneness taking place between the creaturely and divine worlds'.[106] Cioran's reckoning goes on:

The Making of a Sophiological Philosopher

> In tallying up the aspects of Sophia's hypostases it is impossible ... not to include practically every stage in Solov'ev's rational scheme for transforming all of Christendom. She expresses the unique relationship of the indivisible three-in-One nature of the Godhead; God has Sophia before him in creating the extra-divine world; the World Soul is the potential material or corporeal expression of Sophia's manifested oneness which can become purified and elevated to an identity with her; she is implicit in the three successive manifestations of God's incarnation through Christ, the Holy Virgin and consequently the Church which the natural man, natural woman and society, or collective humanity, have as a divine archetype before them; her mode of operation is 'true love' which is attached to the Divine feminine and which operates potentially in every single feminine individual on earth; finally the ultimate and perfect incarnation of the Divine wisdom receives its complete expression in the reunion of perfect humanity with God in God-manhood.[107]

With such a plethora of themes, it is not surprising that commentators from a literary or philosophical background have had trouble in synthesizing Solov'ëv's multifarious statements about Sophia.[108] Cioran is a highly competent Russianist, but though he usually treats theological themes with respect, he is not a theologian and his own religious opinions, if any, are obscure. Balthasar was a Catholic theologian and, though not a Russianist, a discriminating student of metaphysics. Might he assist? Sophia, wrote Balthasar, is 'the essence of the world, gradually moulded, elevated, purified, emerging in its proper selfhood in the primordial image of the Church, the *Panagia*, the spotless virgin and mother of Christ [i.e. Mary the *Theotokos*, or Godbearer], but then broadening out to become the real principle of all the whole of redeemed humanity and creation'.[109] This evaluation, for all its merits, does not do justice to the way that Sophia for Solov'ëv (and, with greater theological control, for Bulgakov) is not *simply* on the created side of the distinction between Uncreated and created. As Cioran's summary makes plain, Sophia is also on the uncreated side, the side of the transcendent God. This is not necessarily confusing, much less obfuscating. William Desmond wrote, 'Why not a name for a community of wisdom and love *between* the God beyond the whole and the divine-human community coming to be within the finite whole?'[110]

To which a partial answer might run: in the Latin West we already have such a name, or, to be more precise, two of them. At the level of what the French Oratorian Louis Bouyer, a student of the sophiologists, would call 'supernatural superexistence' (*surexistence*),[111] that name is 'grace'. At the level of natural existence, the name is 'being'. Being and grace have both Uncreated and created poles. Unless that were so, divine presence—as Creator and Sanctifier—could not combine transcendence with intimacy. Without even using the noun-form 'Sophia' one could say, then, of the commonwealth of being and the communion of grace that these are *sophianic* realities, realities of the 'between'. Such an affirmation would be in accord with Solov'ëv's spirit—but not, as the succeeding chapters will attest, with the letter of his texts. There is, however, one sophiology-friendly feature of Western Catholic thought which retains its salience, when the tasks performed by the language of grace and the language of being are suitably acknowledged. And that is the notion of 'exemplar causality' inseparable from the 'participation metaphysics' of Thomas Aquinas.[112]

The forms of worldly realities have their exemplars—their archetypes—in the divine Ideas. It is an aspect of the thought of Thomas minimized by those who do not care to recognize that he is as much a neo-Platonic thinker as an Aristotelian one—and minimized unduly. Meanwhile the quest for Solov'ëv's Sophia goes on.

NOTES

1. Serge M. Solowiew, *Vie de Vladimir Solowiew par son neveu* (Paris: Éditions SOS, 1982), p. 23.
2. Maxime Herman, *Vie et œuvre de Vladimir Soloviev* (Fribourg: Éditions universitaires, 1995 [1947]), pp. 5–6.
3. Jonathan Sutton, *The Religious Philosophy of Vladimir Solovyov. Towards a Reassessment* (London: Macmillan, 1988), p. 17.

4. Barbara Reynolds, *Dante. The Poet, the Political Thinker, the Man* (London and New York: I. B. Tauris, 2006), pp. 5–6; see also Wendy Elgersma Helleman, *Solovyov's Sophia as a Nineteenth Century Russian Appropriation of Dante's Beatrice* (Lewiston, NY: Edwin Mellen Press, 2010).
5. Dmitri Strémooukhoff, *Vladimir Soloviev et son œuvre messianique* (Lausanne: L'Âge de l'homme, 1975), p. 20.
6. Cited in Samuel D. Cioran, *Vladimir Solov'ev and the Knighthood of the Divine Sophia* (Waterloo, Ontario: Wilfrid Laurier University Press, 1977), p. 48.
7. Hans Urs von Balthasar, *The Glory of the Lord. A Theological Aesthetics, III. Studies in Theological Style: Lay Styles* (Edinburgh: T. & T. Clark, 1986), p. 290.
8. Cioran, *Vladimir Solov'ev*, p. 53. When Solov'ëv, as poet, does not describe her appearance in terms of golden light, he calls it 'azure'. Blue is the heraldic colour of the Virgin Mary, though it may also be colour-coded for revelation-disclosures more widely.
9. *Ibid.*, p. 62.
10. *Ibid.*
11. *Ibid.*, p. 66.
12. *Ibid.* For an alternative view of the 'Legend' as a humorous self-parody, see Judith Deutsch Kornblatt, 'Soloviev on Salvation. The Story of the "Short Story of the Antichrist"', in Judith Deutsch Kornblatt and Richard F. Gustafson (eds.), *Russian Religious Thought* (Madison, WI: University of Wisconsin Press, 1996), pp. 68–87.
13. As relayed in his nephew's biographical study, Sergeï Mikhailovich Solov'ëv, *Zhizn' i tvorcheskaya évolyutsiya Vladimira Solov'ëva* (Brussels: Zhizn' s Bogom, 1997), p. 59.
14. For an excellent account of Solov'ëv's view of the history of philosophy, from the ancients to Hegel, see Thomas Nemeth, *The Later Solov'ëv. Philosophy in Imperial Russia* (Cham: Springer, 2019), pp. 73–96.
15. Herman, *Vie et œuvre de Vladimir Soloviev*, p. 10, n. 8. *Unitotalité* conveys the sense of the Russian word that recurs so often in Solov'ëv's philosophical writing, *vseedinstvo*, 'all-in-one-ness'.
16. S. L. Frank (ed.), *A Solovyov Anthology* (London: SCM Press, 1950), p. 10.
17. Solowiew, *Vie de Vladimir Solowiew*, p. 15.
18. William Desmond, 'God beyond the Whole: Between Solov'ëv and Shestov', in his *Is there a Sabbath for Thought? Between Religion and Philosophy* (New York: Fordham University Press, 2005), pp. 167–99, and here at p. 167.
19. Herman, *Vie et œuvre de Vladimir Soloviev*, p. 13.

20. *Ibid.*
21. Strémooukhoff, *Vladimir Soloviev*, p. 26.
22. Paul Ricœur, *The Symbolism of Evil* (New York, NY: Harper and Row, 1967 [1960]).
23. Keith Lemna, *The Apocalypse of Wisdom. Louis Bouyer's Theological Recovery of the Cosmos* (Brooklyn, NY: Angelico Press, 2019), p. 142, with an internal citation of Louis Bouyer, *Cosmos. The World and the Glory of God* (Petersham, MA: St Bede's Press, 1988), pp. 83–4.
24. Anselm, *Proslogion*, 4, in Benedicta Ward, SLG (ed.), *The Prayers and Meditations of St Anselm with the 'Proslogion'* (London: Penguin, 1986 [1973]), p. 246.
25. Thomas Aquinas, *Summa theologiae*, Ia., q. 45, a. 1, corpus, in Thomas Gilby, OP, *St Thomas Aquinas, Summa theologiae, 8. Creation, Variety and Evil [Ia.44–9]* (London: Blackfriars, 1967).
26. For a subtle juxtaposition of the two 'models' of emanation and making or artistry, see David B. Burrell, 'Act of Creation with its Theological Consequences', in Thomas Weinandy, Daniel Keating and John Yocum (eds.), *Aquinas on Doctrine. A Critical Introduction* (London and New York: T. & T. Clark, 2004), pp. 27–44.
27. Desmond, 'God beyond the Whole', p. 169.
28. Frederick Copleston, SJ, *Philosophy in Russia. From Herzen to Lenin and Berdyaev* (Tunbridge Wells: Search Press, 1986), pp. 49–59.
29. Strémooukhoff, *Vladimir Soloviev*, p. 26. Cf. Ivan V. Kireevsky, 'On the Necessity and Possibility of New Principles in Philosophy', in Peter K. Christoff, *An Introduction to Nineteenth Century Russian Slavophilism, II. I. V. Kireesvkij* (The Hague: Mouton, 1972), pp. 346–75.
30. Ivan V. Kireevsky, 'On the Nature of European Culture and its Relation to the Culture of Russia', in Marc Raeff (ed.), *Russian Intellectual History. An Anthology* (Atlantic Highlands, NJ: Humanities Press, 1978 [1966]), pp. 175–207.
31. Cited from his letters (E. L. Radlov, ed., *Pis'ma Vladimira Sergeevicha Solov'ëva*, St Petersburg, Obshchestvennaya Pol'za, 1908–12, 4 volumes), III, pp. 105–6, in Strémooukhoff, *Vladimir Soloviev*, p. 28.
32. For an impressive series of parallels, both Christological and cosmological, see Richard F. Gustafson, 'Soloviev's Doctrine of Salvation', in Deutsch Kornblatt and Gustafson, *Russian Religious Thought*, pp. 45–7. 'Soloviev reshapes the medieval and monastic elements of Maximus' Chalcedonian reworking of the Eastern Christian tradition from Origen and the Cappadocians through Pseudo-Dionysius into a nineteenth-century

philosophical theology expressed in the language not of Greek patristics but of German idealism, and addressed not to monks but to the intellectual elite and Church leaders of the divided inhabited world of Russian and the West. The great Eastern Christian doctrine of salvation as deification was thereby transformed from a monastic justification for the contemplative life into a grand moral, ecumenical and cosmological scheme designed to restore the "faith of our fathers" to modern man', ibid., p. 47.

33. Abbott Gleason, *European and Muscovite: Ivan Kireevsky and the Origins of Slavophilism* (Cambridge, MA: Harvard University Press, 1972), pp. 236–57.

34. Marina Kostalevsky, *Dostoevsky and Soloviev: The Art of Integral Vision* (New Haven and London: Yale University Press, 1997), p. 10. Solov'ëv's *Filosofskie nachala tesl'nogo zananiya (The Philosophical Principles of Integral Knowledge*, written in 1877), is indebted for its intellectual direction to Kireevsky's 1856 treatise of the same name.

35. 'Mifologicheskiĭ protsess v drevnem yaz'ichestve', in S. M. Solov'ëv and E. M. Radlov (eds.), *Sobranie sochineniĭ Vladimira Sergeevicha Solov'ëva* (St Petersburg: Prosveshchenie, 1911–14), I, pp. 1–26.

36. Copleston, *Philosophy in Russia*, p. 25.

37. Marie-Elise Zovko, *Natur und Gott. Das wirkungsgeschichtliche Verhältnis Schellings und Baaders* (Würzburg: Königshausen und Neumann, 1996).

38. For Solov'ëv's complex relation to Schelling, see Paul Valliere, 'Solov'ëv and Schelling's Philosophy of Revelation', in Wil van den Bercken, Manon de Courten, Evert van der Zweerde (eds.), *Vladimir Solov'ëv: Reconciler and Polemicist* (Leuven: Peeters, 2000), pp. 120–9.

39. Strémooukhoff, *Vladimir Soloviev*, p. 30.

40. Cited *ibid.*, p. 29, from Solov'ëv and Radlov, *Sobranie sochineniĭ*, I, pp. 10–11.

41. *Krizis zapadnoĭ filosofii (Protiv pozitivistov)*, in Solov'ëv and Radlov, *Sobranie sochineniĭ*, I, pp. 27–170. There is an English translation: *The Crisis of Western Philosophy: Against the Positivists* (Hudson, NY: Lindisfarne Press, 1996).

42. Thomas Nemeth, *The Early Solov'ëv and his Quest for Metaphysics* (Cham: Springer, 2004), p. 15.

43. *Ibid.*, p. 18.

44. *The Crisis of Western Philosophy*, p. 131.

45. Nemeth, *The Early Solov'ëv*, p. 27.

46. *The Crisis of Western Philosophy*, p. 11.

47. *Ibid.*, p. 141.

48. Herman, *Vie et œuvre de Vladimir Soloviev*, p. 26; cf. Vladimir Soloviev, *Crise de la philosophie occidentale* (Paris: Aubier, 1947), pp. 342–3. As Desmond points out, Solov'ëv gives the impression that 'the original *ontological guilt of being* finds expression in the self-affirmation of the individual against the whole. 'Salvation from evil consists in the sacrifice of this false absoluteness and submission to the truth of the immanent movement of the whole towards the consummating "All-unity" which will be all in all': thus 'God beyond the Whole', p. 178, where italics are original. Solov'ëv's younger contemporary Lev Shestov (1866–1938) decried *vseedinstvo* (sarcastically, 'omnitude') as a danger to the person. 'Singular selfhood is a kind of world unto itself, not a mere moment of a larger whole … The dialectical language of parts and wholes is not fully fitting for this idiotic intimacy', *ibid.*, p. 196.
49. Nemeth, *The Early Solov'ëv*, p. 31.
50. *Ibid.*, citing *The Crisis of Western Philosophy*, p. 138.
51. *The Crisis of Western Philosophy*, p. 140.
52. Nemeth, *The Early Solov'ëv*, pp. 39–48.
53. Marc Raeff, 'Enticements and Rifts: Georges Florovsky as Russian Intellectual Historian', in Andrew Blane (ed.), *Georges Florovsky. Russian Intellectual and Orthodox Churchman* (Crestwood, NY: St Vladimir's Seminary Press, 1993), pp. 219–86, and here at pp. 273–4.
54. Zdenek V. David, 'The influence of Jakob Boehme on Russian Religious Thought', *Slavic Review*, 21.1 (1962), pp. 43–64.
55. Nemeth, *The Early Solov'ëv*, p. 48. Nemeth's lack of empathy might be ascribed to his indifference to theology, His last word on Solov'ëv is to the effect that his 'main contribution may well have been [a] transposition of ethical and ontological concerns from the religious sphere to the secular', Nemeth, *The Later Solov'ëv*, p. 298.
56. Strémooukhoff, *Vladimir Soloviev*, p. 42.
57. *Ibid.*, pp. 42–3.
58. 'Lady Wisdom, or Sophia was decidedly a focus of interest for esoteric kabbalist thought, a mystic tradition and school of thought within Judaism which can be traced back to post-exilic developments represented by the Book of Jubilees, and Essene teachings. According to Gershom Scholem, Kabbalah developed from Jewish speculation on the Genesis account of creation and Ezekiel's vision of the Divine Throne in the Talmudic era, interacting with Gnostic thought of the early centuries of our era', Helleman, *Solovyov's Sophia*, p. 29.
59. Strémooukhoff, *Vladimir Soloviev*, p. 43. 'Malkuth' would seem to correspond, he suggests, to the Baroque-period Lutheran kabbalist Jakob

The Making of a Sophiological Philosopher

Boehme's 'divine virgin Sophia', though the active element of Wisdom undertaking progressive incarnation with a view to a final consummation seems absent in Boehme's disciples, and is perhaps more likely to be found in a Jewish context, *ibid.*, n. 22.

60. Cited from his preface to D. Ginsbourg, 'Kabbala, misticheskaya filosofiya évreev', *Voprosÿ filosofii i psikhologii*, III.33 (1896), p. 279, Strémooukhoff, *Vladimir Soloviev*, p. 42.
61. Lemna, *The Apocalypse of Wisdom*, pp. 191–225.
62. Strémooukhoff, *Vladimir Soloviev*, p. 46; for the conflicting opinions of Solov'ëv's nephew and Bulgakov see *ibid.*, n. 36.
63. Cited in Nemeth, *The Early Solov'ëv*, p. 52.
64. Solowiew, *Vie de Wladimir Solowiew*.
65. *La Sophie et les autres écrits français* (Lausanne: La Cité, 1978), p. 3.
66. *Ibid.*, p. 4.
67. *Ibid.*, p. 5.
68. Nemeth, *The Early Solov'ëv*, p. 62.
69. *Ibid.*
70. von Balthasar, *The Glory of the Lord*, p. 295.
71. See Cioran, *Vladimir Solov'ev*, pp. 41–2, for these biographical claims.
72. Smith, *Vladimir Soloviev and the Spiritualization of Matter*, p. 6.
73. Cioran, *Vladimir Solov'ev*, p. 32.
74. *Ibid.*, p. 43.
75. Andrzej Walicki, *A History of Russian Thought. From the Enlightenment to Marxism* (Oxford: Clarendon, 1988), p. 392.
76. Cioran, *Vladimir Solov'ev*, p. 47.
77. 'Tri sily', in Solov'ëv and Radlov, *Sobranie sochineii*, I, pp. 227–39.
78. Paul Valliere, *Modern Russian Theology. Bukharev, Soloviev, Bulgakov. Orthodox Theology in a New Key* (Edinburgh: T. & T. Clark, 2000), p. 114.
79. Nemeth, *The Early Solov'ëv*, pp. 69–70.
80. *Filosofskie nachala tsel'noeznaniya*, in Solov'ëv and Radlov, *Sobranie sochineniĭ*, I, pp. 250–407.
81. Herman, *Vie et œuvre de Vladimir Soloviev*, p. 40.
82. Strémooukhoff, *Vladimir Soloviev*, p. 53.
83. Nemeth, *The Early Solov'ëv*, p. 79.
84. *Ibid.*, p. 81.

85. *The Principles of Integral Knowledge* (Grand Rapids, MH: Eerdmans, 2008), pp. 113–14.
86. *Ibid.*, p. 121.
87. Cited by Nemeth, *The Early Solov'ëv*, p. 91.
88. Michael Aksionov Meerson, 'The Retrieval of Neoplatonism in Solov'ëv's Trinitarian Synthesis', in van den Bercken, de Courten and van der Zweerde, *Vladimir Solov'ëv*, pp. 233–49, and here at p. 248.
89. Aidan Nichols, OP, *From Hermes to Benedict XVI. Faith and Reason in Modern Catholic Thought* (Leominster, 2009), pp. 48–67.
90. Aquinas had spoken of 'adaptations', 'plausible arguments (*rationes*)', 'probable arguments (*persuasiones*) but not demonstrations—see Gilles Emery, 'The Doctrine of the Trinity in St Thomas Aquinas', in Weinandy, Keating and Yocum, *Aquinas on Doctrine*, pp. 45–66, and here at p. 47.
91. See, for instance, Hans Urs von Balthasar, *Cosmic Liturgy. The Universe according to Maximus the Confessor* (San Francisco: Ignatius, 2003), pp. 115–36.
92. *Ibid.*, p. 117.
93. Cited *ibid*, p. 131.
94. *Ibid.*, p. 120.
95. Strémooukhoff, *Vladimir Soloviev*, p. 57.
96. *Ibid.*
97. For a rare reference, see Sergius Bulgakov, *The Wisdom of God. A Brief Summary of Sophiology* (New York and London: Williams and Norgate, 1937), p. 215, in connexion with the 'Whore of Babylon' of Apocalypse 17:5.
98. G. C. Stead, 'The Valentinian Myth of Sophia', *Journal of Theological Studies*, ns 20 (1969), pp. 75–104.
99. A danger not entirely avoided in Maria Carlson, 'Gnostic Elements in Soloviev's Cosmology', in Deutsch Kornblatt and Gustafson, *Russian Religious Thought*, pp. 49–67. Her comparison of Solov'ëv, most of whose prose work is philosophically controlled, to Mme Helena Blavatsky indicates Carlson's focus on the esoteric, as explored in her *'No Religion Higher than Truth': A History of the Theosophical Movement in Russia, 1875–1922* (Princeton, NJ: Princeton University Press, 1993). Neo-Buddhist Solov'ëv is not—though Maria Carlson's comparison between Late Antique discontents and the *fin-de-siècle* epoch is telling; see her 'Gnostic Elements in Soloviev's Cosmology', p. 53.
100. F.-M. Sagnard, *La Gnosie valentienne et le témoignage de saint Irénée* (Paris: Vrin, 1947).

101. Valliere, *Modern Orthodox Theology*, p. 265.
102. Sergius Bulgakov, *The Lamb of God* (Grand Rapids, MI: Eerdmans, 2008), pp. 444–5.
103. Lemna, *The Apocalypse of Wisdom*, p. 173.
104. Bulgakov, *The Wisdom of God*, p. 84.
105. *Ibid.*, p. 74.
106. Cioran, *Vladimir Solov'ev*, pp. 22–3.
107. *Ibid.*, p. 36.
108. Helleman, *Solovyov's* Sophia, pp. 19–20.
109. von Balthasar, *The Glory of the Lord*, p. 292.
110. Desmond, 'God beyond the Whole', p. 181.
111. See, for example, Louis Bouyer, *The Church of God. Body of Christ and Temple of the Spirit* (San Francisco, CA: Ignatius, 2011), p. 530.
112. Cornelio Fabro, *Participation et causalité selon S. Thomas d'Aquin* (Louvain: Publications universitaires de Louvain, 1961), the classic modern study. One might add that in the Greek tradition, for instance, in St Maximus, a similar 'metaxological' term would be *logoi*—qua volitional thoughts in the divine mind they are uncreated, whereas qua the intelligible principles of creaturely things they are created. See 'betweenness' renders the universe open to Christological reunification: see Torstein Tollofsen, *The Christocentric Cosmology of St Maximus the Confessor* (Oxford: Oxford University Press, 2008).

✢ 2 ✢

The Theosophy Project

In *The Critique of Abstract* [or 'Detached'] *Principles* (1877–80), Solov'ëv continued the line already set forth in his study of Western philosophy's historic 'crisis'.[1] The title gives the game away. Like *The Crisis of Western Philosophy* and the later *The Philosophical Principles of Integral Knowledge*—but at much greater length than either (the book consists of 46 chapters, with preface and conclusion), *The Critique of Abstract* [or 'Detached'] *Principles* is an assault on 'exclusivisms', understood as principles formulated defectively on the basis of fragmentary aspects of human nature, rather than human nature in its wholeness. The two chief 'abstract' (or 'detached') principles Solov'ëv describes are 'realism', understood as empiricism—and, therefore, in effect, phenomenalism—and, once again, 'rationalism'. As he writes, 'The critique of these abstract (and in their abstractness) false principles must consist in defining their particularity and demonstrating the internal contradiction into which they fall when they try to take the place of the whole'—for Solov'ëv's criterion of judgment is, as always, *vseedinstvo*, spiritual uni-totality.[2] The limitations of these principles suggest the need to invoke a further principle, at once complementary and super-ordinate, capable of serving as a foundation for knowledge, morality, aesthetics, to none of which can empiricism or rationalism do justice. A more adequate principle will invoke a divine ground for both things and mind itself. God, *theos*, cannot be left out: hence, as Paul Valliere explains, 'the critique of abstract principles in social and political philosophy generates the ideal of "free *theo*cracy"; in theoretical philosophy, "free *theo*sophy"; in esthetics, "free *theu*rgy"'.[3]

39

So far as 'theosophy' is concerned, the 'thing in itself'—the reality behind the appearances of the world—may be inaccessible to our senses and to the activity of reason alone. But it is not necessarily 'inaccessible to faith,'[4] that is, to an intuition for which the appropriate adjectives are (singly or together) 'mystical' and 'intellectual'. Yet, as Solov'ëv explained towards the close of the epistemological/ontological discussions in the *Critique*, a knowledge of reality that is purely mystical/intellectual in kind would yield at best only the 'absolute being' of the object—that is, its origin in the 'unconditionally Existent', in the ultimate Subject of being, God—and not its 'actual' (its enacted, concrete) being here and now.[5] Thus there arises, quite properly, the requirement for the completion of intuition from the side of reason and experience respectively. Fortunately, man is a subject in his own right endowed with a range of powers, a 'microcosmic reflection of the macrocosmic Subject of all being'.[6] The *Critique* is 'epistemology with an ontological intent', its goal to 'show the inadequacy of all viewpoints other than that of the all-unity',[7] since 'without an interconnected whole, we have no single unity, no truth.'[8] It is not, however, 'the universe taken as a whole [that is] the ultimate or unconditionally existent',[9] but God—even if Solov'ëv did not convince all his contemporaries (or later students) that his presentation had successfully overcome the danger, for an Orthodox Christian, of pantheism. Yet he had never been interested merely in the inter-connectedness of all things, in the manner of the egalitarian eco-theology that surfaced among the Christian churches a century after his death. His was a hierarchical universe where, in the language of Scholastic philosophy, all things are related to God by an *ordinatio ad unum*, an ordering to the One. A satisfactory Christian intellectualism, what Solov'ëv terms a 'free theosophy', will wish to combine philosophy and science with theology, the three disciplines whose root epistemic endowments are, respectively, rationality, sense experience, and intuition.[10]

Some of this is familiar from the earlier treatises. But a great deal of the *Critique* is taken up with ethics. Here comes something new. 'A complete moral theory must pass from the question, "What ought I to do?" to "How is the moral society to be realized?"'[11] The first question shows Solov'ëv's rooting in Kantian ethics, the second question how he goes beyond it. Stressing the universality of the moral law, the 'noumenal' (rather than 'phenomenal' or empirically available) nature of freedom, and the obligation to treat other persons as ends, not means, Solov'ëv aligned himself with Kantian ethics whilst simultaneously holding the latter to be insufficient because incomplete. For Kant had omitted to describe the *organization* of human creatures in a kingdom of ends.[12] The theosophic synthesis is to have its social analogue in 'free theocracy', a society where human beings as moral agents will become aware of the call to 'uni-totality' and be assisted in practising universal solidarity through active sympathy with their neighbours. Just as empiricism and rationalism are not enough in epistemology and ontology, so socialism (for Solov'ëv the highest form of empirical social ethics) and rational legalism are not enough in regard to the structure and ethos of civility. The normative end of society and politics 'must be one which all people can love and which nurtures their love for each other'.[13] All social institutions—including economic organization and the State—must be joined to the love of God, and here a third form of community is needed, a religious association: in brief, the Church.

Is such a 'free theocracy' possible? Is the suggestion plausible, even veracious? Solov'ëv's attempt to answer that question occupies much of the second half of the *Critique*. Solov'ëv opposed the Western Liberal concept of a free Church in a free State. The noun 'theocracy' means what it says. But so does the adjective 'free'. Just as love cannot simply swallow up justice, so the Church, which gives institutional expression to the love of God, cannot displace the State which has its own legitimate remit based on the rule of law. And as justice cannot simply swallow up all other legitimate human concerns and activities in the social order, so the State cannot displace civil society its multifarious occupations and tasks. But these three levels, Church, State, civil society are not simply equals, they are hierarchically inter-related. As he writes, in a society embodying the norm of free theocracy all the various elements of society, all the aspects and spheres of social relations are preserved, and they exist not as isolated, introverted mutually irrelevant fields, or as fields that compete for exclusive dominance, but as necessary parts of one and the same complex entity ... Here we cannot have contradiction and exclusivity between the elements, for if all are necessary to each other, then all are autonomous and also dependent on one another at the same time.[14]

In the closing sections of *The Critique of Abstract Principles* Solov'ëv touches on the importance of human creativity, notably in art, for the full realization of truth. In a transformed sociality, people will seek to realize that uni-totality in the world of matter world by appropriate—let us call it suitably 'sacramental'—embodiment in their natural surroundings. It is this activity to which Solov'ëv gave the name 'free theurgy', coined, plainly enough, on the model of 'free theosophy' and 'free theocracy'.

Morals and the theory of knowledge find their appropriate outcome in the idea of 'uni-totality'. In morals, that will mean the absolute good; in gnoseology, it will mean absolute truth, and when realized in the material order, absolute beauty. Goodness, truth and beauty, are of course three of the 'transcendentals' of Christian Scholasticism, three wide-ranging determinations of created being that show its origin in the Uncreated. Looked at theologically, *The Philosophical Principles of Integral Knowledge* are something of a *praeparatio evangelica* in metaphysical guise.

The *Lectures on Godmanhood*,[15] originally given in early 1878 in St Petersburg to audiences of a thousand, and published over the following three years in the journal *Pravoslavnoe obozrenie* (considerably altered, it is believed, in the case of Lectures XI and XII[16]), throw more light on how Solov'ëv understood the controversial topic of 'Wisdom', at any rate at the time of their delivery.[17] They also give a far better idea of his understanding of Christianity than do the studies in comparative religion and speculative philosophy described in the previous chapter. In a word, they are his most explicitly theological contribution so far. In the last chapter, I looked ahead to some features of Solov'ëv's presentation of Wisdom in this material. Now it is time to consider the *Lectures* for themselves, in more rounded fashion.

The official advertisement for the series, held under the auspices of the 'Society of Friends of Spiritual Enlightenment', ran, in Thomas Nemeth's translation: 'The aim of Mr Soloviev's lectures will be to show the rationality of positive religion, to show that the truth of faith, in the entire fullness of its spiritual content, is at the same time the truth of reason. The central concept of the lectures is the idea of Divine humanity, or the living God.'[18] The finished product could be described by the colloquial English expression 'all over the place'. More elegantly, Valliere calls the *Lectures* 'a colourful philosophical and theological sketchbook'.[19]

Solov'ëv opens by making a straightforward proposal. The 'way toward salvation', parsed as 'the realization of true equality, true freedom and brotherhood'—terms calculated to gain the sympathy of a politically radicalized intelligentsia, will be found in the practice of 'self-denial'. That might seem a mere commonplace of Christian asceticism—until he adds in more philosophical idiom that the only way to self-denial is through exploratory discovery of the drawbacks of self-assertion. By that discovery, or so Solov'ëv maintained, humankind would be led toward 'a conscious and free demand for a union with the unconditional beginning'.[20]

As may be surmised, 'Unconditional Beginning' is one of Solov'ëv's names for God. If and when his prediction for free union with the Beginning is realized, so he told his audience, 'Western humanity will be ready to accept the religious principle, the positive revelation of true religion.'[21] Solov'ëv considered this return to God in a new modality to be the historic vocation of contemporary Russia—and not of any Western country, however advanced. It had been the mission of the West to explore the countryside of self-assertion, to experience pure humanism in both its greatness and its folly. The Western European nations cannot be expected to carry out two historic missions. 'The task of laying the foundation for that religious future is reserved to another.'[22] This was a more diplomatic version of the claim earlier made for the vocation of Russia in the essay 'Three Forces'.

Solov'ëv now turns to that 'Unconditional Beginning' for its own sake. His case for the existence of God has an unusual structure. 'The necessity for an unconditional principle for the higher interests of man—its necessity for the will and the moral activity, for reason and true knowledge, for feeling and creation—this necessity merely renders the actual existence of the divine beginning *probable*, in the highest degree; the complete and unconditional *certainty* of its existence can be given only by faith.'[23] By 'faith' here Solov'ëv means (once again) intuition, or, more expansively, 'mystical intuition'. In *The Philosophical Principles of Integral Knowledge* he had sometimes termed it 'intellectual intuition', itself a commonplace locution among the German Idealists, and the phrase will surface again in the lecture-series. For Solov'ëv, the need for such 'faith' in no way distinguishes belief in God from belief in the independent existence of any reality beyond our own minds. Experience tells us *what* the content of our belief in external realities amounts to, but only faith tells us *that* such realities actually are, rather than consisting of, say, mere phenomena, projections, or even illusions.[24] Plainly, then, Solov'ëv is talking not about theological faith—Christian faith, or its Judaic antecedent, for both of these are faith, specifically, in the self-revealing Word of God. He is speaking of the sort of faith required of any human being who philosophizes, whatever her religion or lack of it. As he explained to his audience, 'The data of experience, *along with the faith in the existence of external objects corresponding to them*, appear as evidence of the actually extant, and as such form the basis of objective knowledge.'[25] Furthermore, for 'the fullness of that knowledge it is necessary that these separate evidences concerning that which exists are connected among themselves, that experience be *organized* into an integrated system; and that is attained by rational thought which gives form to empirical material.'[26] Thus the trio of faith, sense experience, and rational thought constitute the necessary component parts of knowledge. Patently, this is, once again, the 'integral knowledge' of Solov'ëv's master's thesis, and his predecessor among the Slavophiles, Kireevsky.

That is not to say that the analysis so far conducted is without religious application. On the contrary, the same account of how a coherent picture of the world is constructed is perfectly applicable to the unconditional divine Beginning itself. The trio of faith, sense experience and rational thinking re-emerge in new guise. 'Besides religious faith and religious experience, we must also have religious thought, the result of which is the philosophy of religion.'[27]

Here, Buddhism and Christianity, in the way they understand ultimate reality, represent opposing poles. Solov'ëv compares them to the distinct advantage of Christianity. Christian philosophy can do justice to the element of truth in Buddhism, but the converse does not hold. His approach anticipates Balthasar, for whom the truth of divine revelation is exhibited in its ability to integrate within itself all other truth while remaining invincibly resistant to similar incorporation—an affinity the Swiss theologian himself acknowledged in his essay on the Russian philosopher.[28] As Solov'ëv explains,

> The negative religion—the universally-historical expression of which is represented by Buddhism—understands the unconditional beginning as nothing. It is indeed *nothing*, for it is not *something*, it is not any definite, limited being, or a creature among other creatures—for it is above any definition, because it is *free from all*. The freedom from all being (the positive nothingness), however, is not the deprivation [loss] of all being (the negative nothingness) ... Thus the divine beginning, free from all being, from everything, is at the same time and thereby the positive force and power of all being, possesses all, all is its own content; and in that sense *the divine beginning itself is 'all'*. This is indicated in the most general and necessary name which we have to give to the divine beginning—the name of *the absolute*; for the word *absolutum* means, first, *that which is absolved*, i.e. [divested] of all particular definitions; and, second, that which is *fulfilled*, accomplished, completed, i.e. that which possesses all and contains all in itself. At the same time it is evident that both

of these meanings are closely interconnected, so that only in possessing all can one abnegate all.[29]

The proper content of the 'divine beginning' is therefore—to cite a variety of synonymous phrases Solov'ëv uses in the *Lectures*—the 'ideal whole' or 'universal integrity' or 'fulness of being' or the 'positive all'.[30]

Solov'ëv develops the thought that, in the case of relative reality—that which is not absolute reality in its Principle (is not, that is to say, God), the interactions of beings are 'possible only in case those beings have among themselves an essential commonness, i.e. if they are rooted in a single general substance, which forms the *essential medium* of their interaction, embracing all of them in itself but not contained in any one of them separately ... it follows directly that there is an internal connection among all beings, by virtue of which their system appears as the *organism of ideas*.'[31] Here the notion of 'organism of ideas' replaces his earlier scheme of a series of monads enclosed in themselves yet able to relate with each other via their relation with the Absolute, the scheme Solov'ëv took (not without his own 'spin') from Hartmann. Still, the two notions (organism of ideas, series of monads) have obvious affinities.

By 'ideas' here Solov'ëv does not mean 'concepts', any more than he does when he calls the world posited by God as other than his own triune being the divine 'Idea'. By 'idea' in this cosmic context Solov'ëv means the archetypal power which gives something its identity and, especially, its capacity to enjoy intelligible relations with what is not itself. The wider a concept's scope the poorer is its content. Compare the concepts of cat, of animal, of entity, where as we make progress through the list the referents of the terms concerned broaden in number but narrow in their definiteness. With the idea, as contrasted with the concept, the more sharply individualized the scope the richer may well be the content. An idea, claims Solov'ëv, 'develops its own content on different sides and in different directions, realizes itself in different relations; and, consequently, the larger the number of particular ideas with which it is in a direct relation, or the greater number of ideas in its volume, the greater the diversity and definiteness with which it realizes itself, the fuller, the richer is its own content.'[32] Balthasar thought Solov'ëv indebted here to Hegel who had understood the 'law of process ... as the progressive determination of the undetermined, so that by this means determinacy and universality or plenitude develop simultaneously.'[33] But for Solov'ëv the unconditionally full Idea is beyond process, since it can only be in God himself who is fullness of being. Process for Solov'ëv can only mean, then, the 'progressive eschatological embodiment of the Idea in worldly reality.'[34]

Solov'ëv notes how that unconditionality or plenary character must entail not only the unsurpassable richness of the contents of the divine Essence but also, and precisely owing to the character of that Essence, the personality of God—this will be tri-hypostatic personality, if the Absolute is Trinitarian.

> It is obvious, indeed, that Divinity, as the absolute, cannot be *only* a personality, only an 'I', that it is more than a personality. But those who protest against this limitation [treating God as a personality] also fall into an opposite one-sidedness in stating that Divinity is simply *deprived* of personal being, that it is merely an impersonal substance of the all. But if Divinity is substance, i.e. the self-existent, then, as containing all in itself it must differ from all or assert its own being, for otherwise there would be no subject of the containing, and Divinity, deprived of its inward independence, would become not the substance (of all) but merely an attribute of the whole. Thus, in its capacity of substance, Divinity must possess self-determination and cognizance of itself (reflection), i.e. personality and consciousness.[35]

God is not only essence. He is also existence or what Solov'ëv calls the pure Ego, the Existing One, 'I am that I am'. Here, by citing Exodus 3:14, Solov'ëv joins hands, probably unwittingly, with the Thomist school, though the actual phrase the 'metaphysics of Exodus', which conjures up this circle of ideas, had to await the work of Étienne Gilson, who was a mere sixteen year old when Solov'ëv died.[36] For Solov'ëv, the divine 'I' must be the 'sole independent being, which does not admit independent reality in anything else'.[37] What is this but the unique *aseitas* of God so beloved of Thomist Scholasticism?

The personality of divine substance thus established, Solov'ëv can move on to discuss the will of such a God considered as the norm of goodness. The will of God, precisely as absolute, asserts the being and good of all—hence it is to be defined as unconditional grace or love. In Solov'ëv's words, 'The will of God must be the law and norm for the human will not as ratified despotism, but as the cognated (and accepted, chosen) *good*': what is genuinely good for humankind and recognized as such.[38] 'Upon this internal relationship is to be (established) a new covenant between God and mankind, a new divine-human order which is to replace the other, preliminary and transitory, religion which was grounded in the external law.'[39]

The divine will must of its nature, then, seek the universal good of all humanity and not simply that of a single people, Israel. 'If the revelation of God as the exclusive *I* was answered in the people of God also with an exclusive assertion of its own national ego among other nations, then the consciousness to which God revealed Himself as the universal idea, as the all-embracing love, necessarily had to be emancipated from national egoism, necessarily had to become pan-human.'[40] Speaking of the Hebrew prophets Solov'ëv remarks,

> Thus, in the prophetic consciousness, the subjective, purely personal element of the Old Testament Jahve ['I am who I am'] was united for the first time with the objective idea of the universal divine essence. But since the prophets were inspired *men of action*, were practical men in the highest sense of that word, and not contemplative thinkers, the synthetic idea of the divine being was for them more a perception of [their] spiritual sense and the striving of [their] moral will than an object of mental perception. Yet, in order to fill and define with itself the whole consciousness of man, that idea had to become also an object of thought.[41]

The Theosophy Project

The Greek philosophers had made a start. Alexandrian thinkers, both Jewish (Philo) and pagan (Plotinus), had been able to speak not untruly of the 'essence of the divine life ... on the basis of the theoretical idea of a Divinity', but

> in Christianity *the same* all-one divine life appeared as a fact, as an historical reality, in the living individuality of an historical personality. Christians alone came to know the divine Logos and the Spirit, not from the point of view of logical or metaphysical categories, under which they appeared in the Alexandrian philosophy, but for the first time recognized the Logos in their crucified and resurrected Saviour, and the Spirit in the living, concretely experienced, beginning force of their own spiritual regeneration.[42]

The *de facto* historic experience of the infant Church found providentially prepared categories well suited to its philosophical expression.

> As soon as the Christians felt the need of understanding as a universal idea that which they had experienced as a particular fact—they naturally turned toward the intellectual definitions of the Greek and Greco-Jewish thinkers, who had already perceived the theoretical truth of those principles, the manifestations of which (they) the Christians, experienced as a living actuality.[43]

With the help of the early-nineteenth-century German philosophers, it is possible to build further on what the Greeks had achieved. In a footnote where Solov'ëv defends his use of the Germans he writes of the doctrine of God as Trinity:

> For a complete logical explanation of this fundamental dogma, an invaluable means can be found for us in those definitions of pure logical thought, which were so perfectly developed in recent German philosophy which on the formal side have for us the same importance as the doctrines of the Academy and Lyceum had for the ancient theologians; and

those who at present rebel against the introduction of this philosophical element into the domain of religion, would have to deny first the whole past history of Christian theology, which, it may be said, was nourished by Plato and Aristotle.[44]

Developing, or improvising a variation on, the 'demonstration' of the divine Trinity found in *The Philosophical Principles of Integral Knowledge*,[45] Solov'ëv now expounds the doctrine of the triune God in what he regards as the form that is 'most logical', i.e. that best suits 'the requirements of contemplative reason'.[46] He intends to show there are three eternal acts in God, three acts which, by virtue of their own definition, 'reciprocally exclude each other and thus are unthinkable in a *single* subject'; hence

> it is necessary to assume for these three eternal acts *three eternal subjects (hypostases), the second* of which, *being immediately begotten by the first*, is the direct image of its hypostasis, expresses by its actuality the essential content of the first, serves for it as the *eternal expression or the Word; while the third, proceeding from the first, as from the one who has already found its expression in the second*, asserts the second as expressed or in its expression.[47]

What then are the three acts in question?

> God, as the absolute or the unconditional, cannot be content with the mere fact that He has all *in Himself*; He must possess all not only in Himself, but also *for Himself* and *by Himself*. Without such fullness of existence Divinity cannot be completed or absolute, i.e. cannot be God; consequently, to ask, What is the need for God to find Himself in this triune positing of Himself, is the same as to ask: What is the need for God to be God?[48]

Solov'ëv is reiterating how Trinitarianism is a truth of contemplative reason and not just a truth of the Christian Creed. The difference the Gospel events made was that Christians *actually experienced* the Logos incarnate and the Spirit poured forth at Pentecost. It was not that those events served to introduce the *notions* of the Logos and the Spirit for the first time.

Despite his elaborate Trinitarianism, Solov'ëv can also define the content of Christianity as 'singularly and exclusively Christ'.[49] His defence of this statement differs hugely from any standard Christian apologetic. He proceeds by way of four assertions. First, the greater the plurality of elements which the principle of unity of an organism reduces to itself, the more the principle of unity asserts itself. The more universal, the more individual. Hence the absolutely universal is the absolutely individual. So the universal organism, which expresses the unconditional content of the divine Beginning is pre-eminently a peculiar individual being. And this is what we find in the New Adam, Jesus Christ, who integrates all regenerated humanity in himself even as, being as he is the Logos incarnate, all human creatures are in any case related to him as the eternal humanity of God.

The Trinitarian, Christological and anthropological context thus established (if only schematically so), it is time for Sophia to take her bow. Within the Triune God considered as source of the world, the 'acting, unifying beginning, the beginning which expresses the unity of the unconditionally-extant one, obviously is the Word or Logos'.[50] But a unity of a second kind, 'produced unity', receives the name of 'Sophia'.

> If in the absolute we differentiate in general the absolute as such, i.e. as the unconditionally-extant One, from its content, essence, or idea, then we find the direct expression of the first in the Logos, and of the second in Sophia, which is thus the expressed, realized idea. And as the extant One, differing from its own idea is at the same time one with it, so Logos, too, differing from Sophia, is eternally connected with her.[51]

As God Christ must be at once Logos and Sophia, since while in his hypostasis he is the second divine Person, the Word, as one who shares the divine nature with the Father (the *homoousion* doctrine of the Council of Nicaea) he is the bearer of the divine nature, and therefore of the inner world of God—that divine Idea which carries within it the ideas of all things. And in this respect he can be called the 'Wisdom of God', as St Paul did not hesitate to do (I Corinthians 1:24).

Whatever may be thought of Solov'ëv's appropriation of the Pauline Letters for his own purposes, there is, to be sure, an affinity between this lecture and Christian Platonism's notion of the 'Divine Ideas'—the claim that the archetypes of created things exist in God as multitudinous reflections of his own being. Even Thomas Aquinas, often considered the Christian Aristotelian *par excellence*, was Platonist enough to retain this element in patristic metaphysics, derived in his case chiefly from Augustine though he could also have found it, if less compendiously, in his Eastern sources, notably St John Damascene. In an unexpected twist, Solov'ëv argues that the point of this traditional theological claim is not so much to affirm the continuity of God and the world (this would be a natural inference) but to underscore the unique fullness of the divine being, and hence its difference from creation.

> It is precisely in order that God be unconditionally distinguished from our world, from our Nature, from this visible reality, that it is necessary to acknowledge in Him His particular eternal nature, His special eternal world. Otherwise our idea of Divinity will be poorer, more abstract, than our conception of the visible world.[52]

The uniting link between the divine and the natural worlds is inevitably man, man who combines in himself divinity and nothingness. 'There is no need', writes Solov'ëv, 'to dwell on the assertion of this undoubted contrast in man, because it has long represented the common theme of poets as well as of psychologists and moralists.'[53] But at Solov'ëv's hands, anthropology becomes both sophianic and Christological, for in the *Lectures* Christology and anthropology are hardly separable.

> If in the divine being, in Christ, the first or the producing unity is properly the Divinity—God, as the acting force, or Logos—and if, thus, in this first unity we have Christ as the

> divine being proper; then the second unity, the produced one, to which we have given the mystical name of Sophia, is the principle of humanity, is the ideal or normal man. And Christ, as participant in this unity of the human being, is a man, or to use the expression of the Holy Scripture, the second Adam. Thus, Sophia is the ideal or perfect humanity, eternally contained in the integral divine being, or Christ.

—the Logos who took on empirical human nature as Jesus.[54]

For Solov'ëv, the uniqueness of man in his ability synthetically to understand a complex world is only possible if his nature has not only a sophianic foundation but a sophianic identity. And this renders inescapable a special relationship, beyond all other creatures, of humanity with the Logos, even prescinding from the fact of the Incarnation in the Virgin's womb. Solov'ëv does not consider the case of other possible rational species in the universe, a motif which would require considerable adjustments to his argument, calling into question, perhaps, the very notion of 'Godmanhood' (*bogochelovechestvo*) as found in his work.

Evidently, Solov'ëv has moved away from considering the uncreated divine Idea in and for itself. He is now treating it as so structured that, expressed in creation, it establishes a world inherently comprehensible by human beings. That, to Solov'ëv's mind, would not be possible unless there were at the intelligible centre of the Idea what he terms 'primordial humanity'. If God's Idea is his Wisdom, then this Wisdom is poised to be, through the creative act, the form of an 'anthropic' cosmos. It is at this point that the difficulties of theological sophiology arise, for are we now speaking about created wisdom—or uncreated?

Here, three-fourths of the way through the *Lectures*, Solov'ëv takes a further step. Not only is Sophia identical with prototypical humanity. Owing to her relation with the 'world soul', that 'soul' too must enjoy in some manner anthropic form. At one level, that is saying, straightforwardly enough, that the natural cosmos was always ordered to the emergence of its crown and centre, namely, *homo sapiens*. But at another level it is ascribing a quasi-personal agency to the *anima mundi*.

> The divine beginning, inherent in her, liberates her from her created nature, while the latter makes her free in regard to Divinity. In embracing all living beings (souls) and in them also all ideas, she is not exclusively bound to any one among them, is free from all of them—but, being the immediate centre and real unity of all these beings, she receives in them, in their particularity, independence from the divine beginning [and] the possibility of acting upon it in the capacity of a free subject.[55]

When in her self-assertion this world soul underwent separation from the divinity, the unity of cosmic creation broke up into a multitude of separated elements. Solov'ëv rewrites St Paul's letter to the Romans to the effect that at the Fall it was the world soul and not God (or Adam's defaulting, divinely permitted) that 'subjected the creation to vanity' (Romans 8:20).

Building up as Solov'ëv now is to an account of the redemptive Incarnation, he speaks of the world soul as tending innately to the embodiment of the divine in the world. That 'soul' naturally seeks the fullness of being in all-unity. But since by itself the tendency cannot attain its end—the creaturely Sophia can never *become* the Uncreated Sophia—its goal can only be achieved by the direct initiative of God. As Solov'ëv writes,

> In the world... the eternal idea of the absolute organism had to be gradually realized; and the effort toward that realization, the striving towards the incarnation of Divinity in the world—this striving is universal, one in all, and therefore transcends the limits of each—it is this striving which, representing the inner life and beginning of movement in all that exists, that is the world soul, properly speaking. And if... the world soul by herself cannot realize herself because she lacks a definite positive form [necessary] for that purpose, then, it is obvious that in her impetus towards the realization [of the striving]

> she must look for that form in another; and she can find it only in the one who eternally contains that form, i.e. in the divine beginning: which thus appears as the active, formative, and determining principle of the world-process.[56]

The creation of man in God's image and likeness had been the necessary first stage in the economy of the Incarnation. 'In man the world soul for the first time is internally united with the divine Logos in consciousness, as in the pure form of all-unity.'[57] The role of organizing the universe 'which from the beginning belonged to the world soul (as the eternal humanity) receives in the natural man, i.e. [the humanity] that was produced in the world process, the first opportunity of being factually realized in the order of nature'.[58] But the creation of man in God's image and likeness also introduces into creation the possibility of a spurious self-deification on the part of the human, man taking the place of God by arrogant glorying in his own powers.

> Man has not only the same inner essence of life—all-oneness—as God: he is also free to desire to have it as God, i.e. he may of himself wish to be like God ... In order to have it of himself and not only from God, he asserts himself apart from God, outside of God, he falls away and separates himself from God in his consciousness in the same manner as the world soul originally seceded from Him all her being.[59]

The Fall of man is what made the Incarnation not only desirable but necessary.

> In order that the divine beginning could really overcome the evil will and life of man, it is necessary that it appear for the soul a living personal force, able to penetrate into the soul and to take possession of it, it is necessary that the divine Logos should not only influence the soul externally but [that he should] be born within the soul not [only] limiting or enlightening it, but regenerating it. And as the soul in the natural mankind appears actually only in a plurality of the individual souls, the actual union of the divine beginning

with the soul also necessarily assumes an individual form, i.e. the divine Logos is born as an actual individual man.[60]

—Jesus of Nazareth, the 'representative and the head of all regenerated humanity.'[61]

The penultimate and concluding lectures became a single chapter in the printed book. In their final form, they are devoted to the Redeemer's person and work, and to the coming into existence of the Church as his Body. As the Logos, in whose image humanity is made, Christ was always the 'spiritual centre of the universal organism.'[62] But just as humanity, once embroiled in Adam in the realm of phenomena, became through the Fall estranged from both God and nature, so 'Christ also, as the active principle of that unity, for the real restoration of it has to descend into the same stream of phenomena, has to be subjected to the same law of external being, and from the centre of eternity become the centre of history, appearing at a certain moment of it [namely], 'in the fullness of time.'[63]

Solov'ëv understands the redemptive Incarnation as above all a victory over evil, crucially in the days of Jesus' flesh, but finally at the End of all things. The triumph over Satan in the mystery of the Temptation of Christ is almost more prominent than the Passion and Death in Solov'ëv's scheme which is itself preceded by an account of the presuppositions of the union—viz., between God and man in the divine-human personality of the Saviour.

In the ontological composition of the God-man, the union of natures in Christ is not unthinkable so long as we are neither deists nor pantheists. Just as the world, outside of God by dint of limitedness, is united with God in its internal life or 'soul', so God, though in his transcendence utterly beyond the world, is simultaneously related to it as Creator. In this perspective, the Incarnation, though beyond prediction, is far from alien to the general order of things. Moreover, in man a divine element is linked to materiality via a quintessentially distinctively human *tertium quid*—which Solov'ëv defines as identical with the rational mind if the latter be understood as the 'relationship' (a term he links to the root-word *ratio*) of the other two elements or factors.[64] A human being in whom the 'natural man'—knowing himself only as part of material nature—was freely subjected to the divine element might exemplify what Solov'ëv terms 'spiritual humanity'. But for a union of these elements to be 'an actual union of the two beginnings'— the unconditioned Beginning that is God and the conditioned beginning that is empirical humanity, then 'the actual presence of both these beginnings is necessary', and this can only mean two natures entering freely into concord.[65] This new, post-Adamic, 'spiritual man' will be the One whom the Ecumenical Councils of Chalcedon, and Constantinople II and III combine to announce to us in Jesus Christ: 'a single God-man personality, uniting in itself two natures and possessing two wills'.[66]

For the work of this union, the 'free participation and action' of both natures was needful—which means for the human nature, *podvig*, a 'feat' or 'exploit' of self-denial, and for the divine nature, *kenosis*, self-abnegation. Just as, before Christ, natural humanity could 'deny' itself in order to make progress, so in an equally limited manner the Logos had, no doubt, acted upon natural humanity in 'different finite forms of the world life'—and yet, prior to the Enfleshment, such 'cosmic and historic theophanies' in no way affected 'Its inner being or awareness of Itself'.[67] This is where the kenotic Incarnation differs. 'Not that [the divine Beginning] wholly enters into the limits of natural consciousness (that is impossible) but it actually *feels* these limits as *its own at the given moment*'.[68] Such self-limitation of Godhead in Christ allows Jesus's natural human will so to renounce itself in freedom 'in favour of the divine beginning' as to obtain its own 'inner good'.[69] Christ as God had freely renounced the divine glory. In so doing he acquires the possibility of attaining that same glory as man—with a view to human salvation at large.

Hence the crucial importance for Solov'ëv's Christology of the Temptations of Christ. The Temptations are vindications of One who, 'experiencing the limitations of a natural being, ... may be subjected to the temptation to make His divine power a means for the aims which develop as the result of those limitations'.[70] By overcoming the efforts of the Evil One (Solov'ëv writes 'the evil beginning') to 'incline His human will to self-assertion', Christ 'subjected and co-ordinated this human will with the divine will, [thereby] deifying His manhood after the inhumanization of His Divinity'.[71] The twentieth-century Swedish exegete Harald Riesenfeld would provide some support for Solov'ëv's high theology of the temptations of Christ in his *The Gospel Tradition*.[72]

It remained to complete this operation by extending it to man's sensual nature, to the human body. And this was the work reserved for his saving Passion and Death. As Solov'ëv sums up,

> The human beginning, having placed itself in the proper relationship of voluntary subjection to, or accord with, the divine beginning, as its inner good, thereby once more received the significance of the intermediary [or] uniting element between God and nature; and the latter, purified by the death on the cross, lost its material separateness and weight, became a direct expression and instrument of the divine spirit, a true *spiritual body*. It was with that body that Christ arose [from the dead] and appeared to His Church.[73]

That 'due relationship between Divinity and nature in humanity' must now be appropriated by all mankind. This takes place in the incorporation of human beings into Christ's 'body' in a further sense of that word. Here we are thinking of his 'mystical' body—the adjective is not Solov'ëv's own but helps to avoid confusion—the body that is the Church. Solov'ëv adopts a developmental account of the Church which he sees growing from an apostolic embryo. That is because his stress lies on something complex and vast: 'the full realization of the free God–man union in the whole of mankind in all the spheres of its life and activity'.[74] Only as embracing everything—in the supernatural sociology of a 'free theocracy'—can the Church receive its full measure as the body of Christ.[75] The Church, historically speaking, is the body of those who accept Christ—but the acceptance could be just exterior: an acknowledgement of the *de facto* Incarnation and the binding force of the divine commands. It might not be (also) interior, by an 'inward uniting with Christ as the parent of [the] new spiritual life [and] the head of the new spiritual kingdom'.[76] External Christianity, 'believing in the truth of Christ but not regenerated by it', succumbs readily to the third and greatest of Christ's temptations—the temptation to gain the world by worldly means.[77] This was the characteristic crime of the Roman church of the mediaeval epoch, and subsequently of 'Jesuitism'. Solov'ëv does not hesitate to identify its root in 'hidden unbelief', and treat as its give-away sign the hyper-papalism which treats acknowledgement of the pope as more important than 'real confession of the Christian faith'.[78]

The inevitable reaction came in Protestantism, which, however, for lack of any stable criterion of judgment, soon passed into rationalism. By way of a false self-confidence or self-assertion, the West of the Enlightenment and the French Revolution succumbed to the second temptation of Christ: a hubristic confidence in one's own powers independently of God. The impotence of autonomous reason vis-à-vis the realm of the passions explains how 'the kingdom of reason proclaimed by the French Revolution ended in a wild chaos of insanity and violence'.[79]

Absolute rationalism for Solov'ëv is reason abstracting from content, and hence helpless to master life—from which their follows the transition to the first temptation of Christ, the temptation to live by 'bread alone', as rationalism gives way to the empiricism and materialism for which the 'animal nature of man, the material mechanism of the world' are what form the 'true essence of all'.[80] Yet the West ('the Germano-Romanic nations') has not trodden this fateful path to its end. The experience of the deceitfulness of the temptations gives ground for hope, hope that 'Western humanity sooner or later must turn to the truth of Godmanhood'.[81]

The Byzantine-Slav East never set out on this path. It preserved the truth of Christ but, alas, only in the 'soul' not in 'external actuality'—failing to generate a Christian culture comparable in scope to the anti-Christian culture produced by its Western neighbours.

> In the Orthodox Church the enormous majority of its members were captivated into obedience to the truth

through an immediate [direct] inclination, not through a conscious [reflective] process in their inner lives. The really human element, in consequence, proved in the [Eastern] Christian society to be too weak and insufficient for a free and rational carrying out of the divine beginning into the external actuality.[82]

Hence a certain dualism arose between attitudes to God and to the world. The human element developed in the West, however negative its immediate results, was full of promise *if only it could be detached from those results and married to the soul-power of the East*. This is how the 'true society of Godmanhood' can come about, in the image and likeness of the God-man himself.

So Solov'ëv seeks to combine the proper contributions of East and West. 'It is required that society would, first, preserve the divine beginning (the truth of Christ) in all of its purity and, second, develop the principle of human initiative in all its fullness.'[83] The divine element of Christianity preserved in the East could deploy itself fully by making its own the human element developed in the West. For Solov'ëv this cultural project enjoys a mystical and not just an historical meaning. 'If the overshadowing that descended upon the human Mother [Mary] with the active power of God, produced the incarnation of Divinity; then the fertilization of the divine Mother (the Church) by the active human beginning must produce a free deification of humanity.'[84] In these final chapters of the *Lectures on Godmanhood* the language of Sophia has disappeared. Yet there is a sophianic undertow nonetheless, the created wisdom, now purified and elevated in Mary and the Church, 'broadening out to become the real principle of all the whole of redeemed humanity and creation.'[85]

Through the *Lectures on Godmanhood* Solov'ëv began to gain a diverse and distinguished if not numerically enormous audience which included the future metropolitan of Moscow Makariĭ Bulgakov, the novelist Fëdor Dostoevsky, Princess Elizaveta Volkonskaya, hostess of an intellectual salon, and Sofia Khitrova's aunt, the Countess Sofia Tolstoy, widow of the poet and playwright

Alexeï Tolstoy, who was Leo Tolstoy's second cousin—as well as Solov'ëv's own students as 'privat-dozent', a recognized but not salaried assistant professor, in the University of St Petersburg. These were students whom he attracted despite the prevailing climate of philosophical materialism or at least Positivism.

Around 1877–8 Solov'ëv's contact with Dostoevsky intensified (we can see its traces in the analysis of the typical temptation of Western Catholicism, which parallels the novelist's account in the Legend of the Grand Inquisitor in *The Brothers Karamazov*[86]). In July 1878 they went together to the hermitages of Optino, principally to visit a monk with a reputation for holiness and wisdom, the starets Ambrose.

In 'The Startsi of Optino', the third part of a study of 'spiritual fatherhood in Russia in the eighteenth and nineteenth centuries' by two eminent scholars of the twentieth-century Russian diaspora, Vladimir Lossky and Nicolas Arseniev,[87] Lossky describes how the flowering of Russian *starchestvo* (spiritual elderhood) had its origins in the late eighteenth century. It began in the work of Archimandrite Paisiï Velichkovskiï (1722–94) who on the basis of a prolonged stay on Mount Athos renewed monastic life not in Russia itself but in Moldavia, or what is now Romania. The phenomenon of spiritual elderhood continued until the Revolution of 1917—or at least became imperceptible then owing to Bolshevik efforts to eliminate religious belief and practice in Russia.

> Many were the *startsy* in the course of this hundred and fifty years throughout the Russian territory, in the monasteries and the sketes (hermitages), but there was only one Optino, place of predilection where the special grace of *starchestvo* became a local tradition, where a kind of charismatical school formed four generations of *startsy* towards which crowds of people made their way from all the corners of the Empire.[88]

The skete was described faithfully as to its outer appearance by Dostoevsky in *The Brothers Karamazov*.[89]

Lossky and Arseniev explain how eldership worked. 'A starets addresses himself always to a human person, with his unique destiny, his vocation and singular difficulties. By virtue of a special gift he sees each being as God sees him and seeks to help him, by opening his interior sense, without doing violence to his will, so that the human person, liberated from his hidden hindrances, can blossom in grace.'[90] The publication of a life of the starets Paissi in 1846, followed by the systematic editing of translations of patristic texts relevant to the spiritual life, put in close relation the Optino monastery and the literary and erudite world of Moscow. Encouraged by metropolitan Filaret, the starets Makariĭ and his disciples published the ascetical and mystical writings of many of the teachers of the patristic and Byzantine periods.[91] For Makariĭ's client Kireevsky, whom Optino influenced decisively in the generation before Solov'ëv, 'The method of the Fathers must be re-found so as to arouse a new philosophy founded on the Christian tradition, kept intact and living by the Orthodox Church.'[92] 'With Makariĭ the *starchestvo* of Optino enters a new phase of its development, opening itself to the problems of thought, of culture, of the social and political life of Russia. All these questions will be judged by the *startsi* on the spiritual, prophetic, level.'[93]

Finally came Solov'ëv's and Dostoevsky's chosen interlocutor, the starets Ambrose (Alexandr Grenkov, 1812–91).

> To commentators for whom there is little of genuine theological value in Solov'ëv's philosophical thought, the visit would appear to have proved nugatory. Yet even they have to admit that in his 'Legend of the Antichrist', gripped by the apocalyptic anguish that marked the end of his life, Solov'ëv will represent the apostle St John, 'witness' of the Church of the East, come back at the end of time, under the traits of a Russian starets.[94]

As to Dostoevsky: Solov'ëv's ambivalence towards the Catholic Church in the *Lectures on Godmanhood* may owe something to his fellow pilgrim. Their conversations at Optina may have helped Solov'ëv towards identifying Wisdom with the Orthodox Church. Dostoevsky's ardent love of Russia, surpassing that of Solov'ëv's father, and his messianism, which would surely have been alien to Sergeĭ Solov'ëv, could also have influenced him.

But an event which really shook Solov'ëv's faith in the calling of Russia as a Christian people followed on the assassination of Alexander II in March 1881. Two discourses, in the second of which Solov'ëv pleaded for clemency for the perpetrators, criticized Western culture, and affirmed the 'old Slavophile thesis of the Christian truth alive in the soul of the Russian people, adding thereto his own doctrine of Wisdom', went unheeded, at least by the civil authorities.[95] He had aimed to vindicate the Christian character of the monarchical principle in Russia, but the new tsar's response was not only to go ahead with the executions but also to recommend that Solov'ëv temporarily suspend public teaching. Of course, the latter provision was far from draconian. 'It appears that the tsar was disturbed not so much by what Solov'ëv said as by the public's reaction to it. This explains the official advice to Solov'ëv to abstain from public speaking for a time—a measure aimed not against the philosopher himself, but toward the prevention of further political trouble.'[96]

Still only twenty-eight, he never returned to university work. Instead there opened his *Wanderjahre*, where he moved from hotel to hotel, or from the house of one friend to another, his books, papers and clothes distributed between various lodgings. This did not help him in the eyes of the authorities who found suspicious his essentially peregrinating and frequently solitary existence. He himself now considered his 'theosophy' as inefficacious, and began to look for inspiration towards Western Christianity with its practical concern for the construction of the *civitas Dei* by social means.

NOTES

1. *Kritika otvlechennykh nachal*, in Solov'ëv and Radlov, *Sobranie sochineniĭ*, II, pp. v–xvi, 1–397.
2. *Ibid.*, p. 11, translation taken from Valliere, *Modern Orthodox Theology*, p. 121.
3. *Ibid.*, p. 125. Italics added.

4. Herman, *Vie et œuvre de Vladimir Soloviev*, p. 44.
5. *Kritika otvlechennÿkh nachal*, in Solov'ëv and Radlov, *Sobranie sochineniĭ*, II, p. 305.
6. Peter Zouboff, 'Introduction', in Vladimir Solovyev, *Lectures on Godmanhood* (London: Dennis Dobson, 1948), p. 43.
7. Nemeth, *The Early Solov'ëv*, p. 159.
8. *Ibid.*, p. 177.
9. *Ibid.*, p. 181.
10. It looks as though Bulgakov is reflecting this triad in his 1902 essay 'Fundamental Problems of the Theory of Progress', written in criticism of the Russian intelligentsia (notably Positivsts and Marxists) before his return to the Church (in 1907): 'Religion, metaphysical thinking and positive science all answer to fundamental demands of the human spirit, and their development leads to mutual clarification, not destruction', cited by Valliere, *Modern Orthodox Theology*, p. 235. A year later, in 'What does the philosophy of Vladimir Soloviev give the modern mind?', he confessed his debt, answering his own question, 'an integral world-view in which the demands of critical philosophy, metaphysical creativity and natural science are all taken into account and harmonized', cited *ibid.*, pp. 238–9.
11. Nemeth, *The Early Solov'ëv*, p. 142.
12. *Ibid.*, pp. 138–43.
13. Valliere, *Modern Orthodox Theology*, p. 130.
14. *Kritika otvlechennykh nachal*, in Solov'ëv and Radlov, *Sobranie sochineniĭ*, II, p. 185; translation in Valliere, *Modern Orthodox Theology*, p. 133.
15. *Chteniia o Bogochelovechestve*, in Solov'ëv and Radlov, *Sobranie sochineniĭ*, III, pp. 1–181. There are two English translations: *Lectures on Godmanhood* (London: Dennis Dobson, 1948) and *Lectures on Divine Humanity* (Hudson, NY: Lindisfarne Press, 1995).
16. Nemeth, *The Early Solov'ëv*, p. 99. In their oral form these lectures are thought to have contained a critique of the notion of Hell considered too daring for the official censors.
17. In the words of the first translator of the *Lectures* into English, 'This concept of Sophia is perhaps the most changeable in the whole construction of Solovyev's philosophy. It takes on different connotations in different contexts, although its basic meaning remains the same—that of the passive medium through which alone [the] Logos can reduce humanity to divine obedience and deify it, and through it, in it, all created nature', Zouboff, 'Introduction', p. 63.
18. Cited by Nemeth, *The Early Solov'ëv*, p. 97.

19. Valliere, *Modern Orthodox Theology*, p. 144.
20. *Lectures on Godmanhood*, p. 75.
21. *Ibid.*
22. *Ibid.*
23. *Ibid.*, p. 90.
24. One might compare here the notion of 'perceptual faith' in Maurice Merleau-Ponty, *Le Visible et l'invisible* (Paris: Gallimard, 1964), p. 17.
25. *Lectures on Godmanhood*, p. 92. Italics added.
26. *Ibid.* Italics original.
27. *Ibid.*
28. von Balthasar, *The Glory of the Lord*, pp. 183–4.
29. *Lectures on Godmanhood*, p. 103. Italics original.
30. *Ibid.*, pp. 110, 103.
31. *Ibid.*, p. 113. Italics original.
32. *Ibid.*, pp. 114–15.
33. von Balthasar, *The Glory of the Lord*, p. 282.
34. *Ibid.*, p. 283.
35. *Lectures on Godmanhood*, pp. 121–2.
36. Étienne Gilson, *L'Ésprit de la philosophie médiévale* (Paris: Vrin, 1960), pp. 50–1.
37. *Lectures on Godmanhood*, p. 123.
38. *Ibid.*, pp. 124–5.
39. *Ibid.*, pp. 124–5.
40. *Ibid.*, p. 126.
41. *Ibid.*, p. 127. Italics original.
42. *Ibid.*, pp. 127–8. Italics original.
43. *Ibid.*, p. 128.
44. *Ibid.*, p. 129.
45. According to Michael Meerson, all three versions (in *Philosophical Principles of Integral Knowledge*, *Lectures on Godmanhood*, and *Russia and the Universal Church*) share a 'fundamentally Proclean' argumentative structure (abiding, procession, reversion), as first laid out in Proclus' *Elements of Theology*: thus Meerson, 'The Retrieval of Neoplatonism', *passim*.
46. *Lectures on Godmanhood*, p. 129. Italics original.

47. *Ibid.*, p. 138. Italics original.
48. *Ibid.*
49. *Ibid.*, p. 152.
50. *Ibid.*, p.154.
51. *Ibid.*
52. *Ibid.*, p. 155.
53. *Ibid.*, p. 158.
54. *Ibid.*, p. 159.
55. *Ibid.*, pp. 173–4.
56. *Ibid.*, p. 177.
57. *Ibid.*, p. 181.
58. *Ibid.*
59. *Ibid.*, p. 182.
60. *Ibid.*, p. 188.
61. *Ibid.*, p. 191.
62. *Ibid.*, p. 192.
63. *Ibid.*
64. *Ibid.*, p. 194. Solov'ëv understands 'mind' here to include 'will', cf. *ibid.*, p. 198.
65. *Ibid.*, p. 195.
66. *Ibid.*
67. *Ibid.*, p. 196.
68. *Ibid.*
69. *Ibid.*
70. *Ibid.*, p. 197.
71. *Ibid.*, p. 198.
72. Harald Riesenfeld, *The Gospel Tradition* (Philadelphia: Fortress, 1970), pp. 75–93.
73. *Lectures on Godmanhood*, p. 199.
74. *Ibid.*
75. *Ibid.*
76. *Ibid.*, pp. 200–1.
77. *Ibid.*, p. 201.
78. *Ibid.*

79. *Ibid.*, p. 203.
80. *Ibid.*, p. 203.
81. *Ibid.*, p. 204.
82. *Ibid.*, p. 205.
83. *Ibid.*
84. *Ibid.*, p. 206.
85. von Balthasar, *The Glory of the Lord*, p. 292.
86. Thedor [sic] Mikhailovitch Dostoevsky, *The Brothers Karamazov* (London: J. M. Dent, 1927), I., pp. 252–71.
87. Vladimir Lossky and Nicolas Arseniev, *La Paternité spirituelle en Russie au XVIIIème et XIXème siècles* (Bellefontaine: Abbaye de Bellefontaine, 1977).
88. *Ibid.*, pp. 91–2.
89. Dostoevsky, *The Brothers Karamazov*, I., pp. 29–33.
90. Lossky and Arseniev, *La Paternité spirituelle*, p. 109.
91. *Ibid.*, pp. 122–3.
92. *Ibid.*
93. *Ibid.*, p. 125.
94. *Ibid.*, p. 140.
95. Strémooukhoff, *Vladimir Soloviev*, p. 123.
96. Kostalevsky, *Dostoevsky and Soloviev*, p. 88.

✣ 3 ✣

THE THEOCRATIC WRITINGS

AFTER 1881, the union of the churches and the reconciliation of Jews and Christians became Solov'ëv's new priority. The theme was announced in the 1883 essay 'The Great Debate and Christian Politics' and the closing chapters of *The Spiritual Foundations of Life* (1884). It was more fully orchestrated in *The History and Future of Theocracy* (1885–7) and, above all, *Russia and the Universal Church* (1889), the last of which serves too—after the *Lectures on Godmanhood*—as the chief prose source for Solovev's sophiology.

There is an important preamble to these 'theocratic' writings. When the Holy Synod of the Russian Church published a collective letter on the assassination of the tsar-liberator, their text spurred Solov'ëv to write his own encyclical: 'À propos the spiritual power in Russia' (1881). Here he linked what he considered the feeble influence of the Church on Russian society to a rupture between tsar and people, a cleft which should have been overcome by the Orthodox priesthood, the spiritual power *par excellence*. The break-up of unity ascribed by Slavophiles to Peter the Great's reforms Solov'ëv laid at the door of the patriarch Nikon who, fifty years before Peter, had sought to assert his spiritual authority over against the tsardom, seeking to be, like the papal monarchy of the high middle ages, the pinnacle of State power—and, furthermore, its collaborator in persecuting the Old Ritualists ('Old Believers'), by which disaster the Church in Russia lost its moral authority. In 1881 Solov'ëv was thinking along the lines of a local Russian council to make amends. But by 1882 he had began to doubt whether a purely national church could encompass the reconciliation required. Byzantine exclusivism had looked to the past and to one location in space, on the Bosphorus. A church made in its image (the origins, in the Kievan period, of the Church of Russia, were Byzantine) is deprived of universality. A tendency to identify 'Wisdom' with the Church, detectible in what I have called the 'sophianic undertow' to the last of the *Lectures on Godmanhood*, now intensified. But the Church in question had to be more plainly universal than Solov'ëv had thought before. A *centrum universitatis* was indispensable.

In the 1883 essay 'The Great Debate and Christian Politics' Solov'ëv argued that a Christian culture requires both the pious conservation of revealed truth and the robust organization of ecclesiastical activity.[1] The East has only one of these prerequisites, as does the West.

> We know that in this history Christianity appeared as the union and intimate reconciliation of the spiritual cultures of east and west in the truth of the divine humanity. That is why, if one of these elements acquires an exclusive preponderance and absorbs the other, the very character of Christianity finds itself violated in its historic vocation, Christianity ceases to be the expression and incarnation of the idea of divine humanity in universal history.[2]

For Solov'ëv,

> The goal of Christian politics is the union of humanity in the Church of Christ. This goal cannot be attained so long as the visible Church remains divided. That is why the restoration of ecclesiastical unity appears as the primordial task of a Christian politics. But for this work—the union of ecclesiastical collectivities—to have the character of *Christian* politics, it must find its direct origin in religious and moral motives and be ruled by them.[3]

That the motives of participants were political and interested explains the failure of the reunion attempts of Lyons II (1274) and Ferrara-Florence (1438–9)—and, moreover, the degeneration of the papacy (*papstvo*) into 'papism' (*papizm*), the disastrous attempt to consolidate spiritual power by worldly means, including diplomacy and warfare.[4] That was the ground for the hostility to the Western Church of so many Orthodox Russians familiar with the history of their country. Solov'ëv was encouraged by the thought that, nevertheless, the two Communions, Orthodox and Catholic, 'are united in Christ by the apostolic succession, by the true faith and the life-giving sacraments: in that the two Churches do not exclude each other, and form one single unity; that is why the universal Church is one, although *appearing* in two churches'.[5] The question now is how to harmonize their manifestation.

Though Solov'ëv does not say so explicitly in *The Great Debate*, his view of Russia's special vocation had shifted from an earlier theosophical understanding where the task was above all philosophical in character, to a theocratic interpretation where the mission of Russia is to unify the body politic of Christendom and, in that way, to help reestablish the equilibrium of divine humanity. He was encouraged by the fact that Tsar Alexander III had just written to Pope Leo XIII expressing the view that never was the union of Churches and States more necessary for putting an end to the errors which are 'the cause of social malaise' and facilitating a 'return to the holy laws of the Gospel'.[6] Solov'ëv did not entirely neglect Protestantism which, once Orthodoxy and Catholicism had been brought into harmony, would, he thought, contribute its own desirable stress on liberty. It was, after all, a '*free* theocracy' at which he was aiming, not a combination of the most authoritarian features of State Orthodoxy and the contemporary papacy. In the 1884 essay *Judaism and the Christian Question* where Solov'ëv's description of his intended theocracy gives a better idea of the political structure he had in mind, it is plainly 'an unrestricted, albeit ideal-Christian, monarchy', yet 'throughout his work Solov'ëv continually defends personal freedom, religious tolerance and the rights of man'.[7]

Also dating from 1884, *The Spiritual Foundations of Life* does not at first sight appear to be among the theocratic writings.[8] It starts out as a treatise on the ascetic life, stressing free submission to God in prayer (chapter 1, a commentary on the *Pater*), perfect accord with one's neighbour in almsgiving (chapter 2), and an effort of domination over the flesh in fasting (chapter 3). An introduction sets the anthropological scene. Three chapters follow on Christianity, the Church, and 'State and society according to Christ', and culminate in a Christocentric conclusion on 'the example of Christ, the rule of conscience'.[9] Solov'ëv urgently recommends the following of this model in preparation for the Parousia.[10]

The anthropology of *The Spiritual Foundations of Life* is provided in the opening words of the introduction: 'two invisible wings raise the human soul above the rest of nature: the thirst for immortality and the thirst for truth or moral perfection'.[11] These 'wings' are inseparable, for immortal life without perfection is not a good while a perfection subject to ruin and annihilation is not true. The obstacles to rising above the rest of nature in this way are sin and death—and these too are inseparable, for our nature is fallen. Our conscience judges good and evil, showing thereby in what fallen nature must be corrected but not how to do it: here Solov'ëv was inspired by the Letter to the Romans (7:5–24). For reformation of the self another principle of life is needed, and this is grace, *blagodat*, the 'good gift', higher than the world, for its direct source is God. The gift of grace creates the holy warfare of which prayer, almsgiving and fasting are the three great weapons available to human collaboration in the transformation of the will, 'the three fundamental works of personal religious life, the three bases of personal religion'.[12] Each requires the others for its authenticity.

The lengthy chapter on 'Christianity' which follows is an apologia for the Incarnation in the situation of fallen man as set out in this anthropological introduction.

> In order that the divine principle should truly triumph over the bad will and the life of man, it must manifest itself for the soul as a living and personal force, capable of penetrating it and possessing it. The divine Logos must exercise over the soul not only an exterior influence; it must be born in the soul

itself, it must not confine itself to limiting it and enlightening it, it must regenerate it.[13]

Just as the first Adam was not simply an individual but a synthesis of natural humanity, a pan-human figure, so is the second Adam 'the spiritual centre of the universal organism'.[14] The fact of the Incarnation—*that* the Word became human—fits in with the general meaning of universal evolution and the wider pattern of divine activity therein. But this does not answer the question of the *how*, the character of the union itself, or what Solov'ëv calls the 'mutual action of the divine and natural human principles in the theandric personality'.[15] For this union to be real there must be 'a sole divine-human person, reuniting in itself [sic] the two substances and possessing their wills', Solov'ëv's attempt to sum up the Christological councils of the ancient Church, from Nicaea I to Nicaea II.[16] It is a reprise of what he had already written in the *Lectures on Godmanhood*.

For this union, an act of renunciation is required for both the divine and the human principles in Christ. First of all, the divine must humble itself to accept the limits of the condition of a servant, though Solov'ëv is quick to add, 'not that [God in Christ] is enclosed in these limits, which is impossible, but that he experiences them as his own at any given moment by an active energy on his part'.[17] Then the humanity must renounce the following of its natural will in favour of the divine principle at work in it.[18] The twofold awareness of the God-man, the theandric personality of the Logos incarnate, makes possible the Temptations of Christ where the Saviour faced and overcame Satan's insidious suggestion to 'make of his divine power a means to attain the ends that exceed [the] limits [of his natural existence as human]'.[19] Once again the Temptations are crucial. On an iconostasis designed by Solov'ëv the episode of the Temptations of Christ, one muses, would take centre place.

On Solov'ëv's wider anthropology, which works with three principles in sophianic man—divine, material, and specifically human—the mystery of the Temptations, succeeded and completed by the mystery of the Passion and Death, furnishes the key to the work of salvation.

> The human principle, by placing itself in a suitable relation of voluntary submission in regard to the divine principle considered as the plenitude of its good becomes by that very fact, once again [i.e. after Eden] the mediating and unifying principle between God and nature, since the latter, purified by the death of the cross, loses its character of material particularity and its heaviness and becomes the direct expression and instrument of the divine Spirit, becomes the true *spiritual body* of the risen God-man.[20]

By his life, death and resurrection, Christ has 'revealed that God incarnate in him, is above law and reason, that he can do much more than extinguish evil by his power or unmask it by his light, that, infinite Spirit of life and love, he regenerates and saves the nature which moves in perdition, for he transforms its lies into truth and its perversity into goodness, finding his glory in this act of victorious love'.[21]

The 'new religion', Christianity,

> cannot be only a passive veneration of God (*theosebeia*), or a simple worship (*theolatreia*), but must become an activity in God and with him (*theourgia*), that is to say a conjoint action of God and man, so as to transform carnal or natural humanity into a spiritual or divine humanity ... Humanity as reunited once again to its divine principle in Christ—the Church—is the living body of the divine Logos incarnate, that is, individualized historically in the divine-human personality of Jesus Christ.[22]

In time to come, this will involve the extension of the theandric union to the whole of humanity in all the realms of life and activity in a free theocracy by which the Church will attain the full measure of the 'age' of Christ (cf Ephesians 4:13).[23] In ecclesiology, 'body' is no metaphor but a metaphysical principle, so the growth is real, aided by the Spirit. Solov'ëv insists on the holiness of the Church, made possible by drawing its life and power from its Head by the mediation of the Mother of God and the 'whole invisible Church of the saints'.[24] The instruments of the sanctifying action are threefold: the hierarchical succession (the way), faith in the dogmas, specifically of the divine-humanity (the truth), the sacraments (the life). In the historic Church awareness of these three dimensions moves from latency to clarity—Solov'ëv's version of doctrinal development. 'Before Christianity, it was human nature (the old Adam) that was the stable foundation of life—the divine element was a principle of modification, movement, progress. Contrarywise, after Christianity, it is the divine element, since it is incarnated, that become this stable foundation for our life'.[25]

Thereafter Christification is pursued on two tracks: personal moral perfection and the amelioration of social relations. The latter, of course, renders theocracy imperative. In regard to the State, Christianity comes to save the world so must save its highest expression, the State, by showing the latter the true goal of its existence: to spread Christianity in the world, to work for the pacific *rapprochement* of peoples within Christendom, and to organize social relations in conformity to the Christian ideal of each people.[26] Clearly enough, *The Spiritual Foundations of Life* had achieved the status of a theocratic writing when it drew to its end.

Only enough of *The History and Future of Theocracy* was published (originally, as with so much of Solov'ëv's writing, in a series of articles, this time in *Pravoslavnoe obozrenie*) to amount to a single printed book,[27] unless, that is, one regards *La Russie et l'Église universelle* as, in effect, the compressed completion of his planned three volume work. In the preface, Solov'ëv gives as his aim to 'show that this ancient faith [Russian Orthodoxy], freed from local exclusivism and national egoism, corresponds to eternal and universal truth'.[28] The first two volumes of the projected work would consider respectively 'the philosophy of biblical history' and 'the philosophy of ecclesiastical history', and these were to form the basis for a third volume on the problem of theocracy now.

What survives of *The History and Future of Theocracy* is only a torso, corresponding largely to the first of these subdivisions.

Indeed it chiefly concerns the Old Testament which provided for the future the seed of 'theocracy'. Solov'ëv explains that a theocracy can only exist by virtue of a freedom that submits, a reason that finds truth in authority, and the aspiration of the heart to a perfect life. The human being is the only creature who possesses these indispensable 'theocratic qualities'.[29] Man is

> created after the image and likeness of God, which means after the idea of divinity itself. This idea is uni-totality, since God, being one, possesses all. Man, without possessing all, can, however, receive it from God. This possibility is the image of God in man, while its realization is the likeness ... The universal history is nothing other than the purification and perfecting of the human being in view of theocracy.[30]

Solov'ëv finds the Church to be the 'global organization of true life':[31] divine-human life where eternity is realized in time, divine love in human freedom. He agrees with the early Slavophiles in their account of the Church as a 'living organism of truth and love', but disagrees with their exclusion of the whole of the West from this same organism—by which exclusion they themselves fell away from ecclesial love into 'confessional egoism.'[32]

The call of Abraham is crucial for Solov'ëv's understanding of the theocratic preoccupations of Scripture. Abraham is elected as a new beginning after the collapse, at Babel, of the attempt to create universal brotherhood on the basis of 'anthropocracy', *chelovekovlastie*. God the master-builder sets in place the cornerstone of a global temple, since in Abraham 'all generations will be blessed' (Genesis 12:3). Making use of a first-century pseudepigraphical text *The Apocalypse of Abraham*—known only in Slavonic, its theme was the status and destiny of Israel—Solov'ëv found foreshadowed in the Book of Genesis the transition from a national theocracy in Israel to a universal theocracy in Christ. In the act of sacrifice described at Genesis 15:9, Abraham is asked to prepare a heifer, a she-goat and a ram, as well as a turtle dove and a pigeon. For Solov'ëv, donning the mantle of those allegorical exegetes, Philo and the Alexandrian fathers, the animals named symbolize the religious awareness of respectively the East (India, Iran and Egypt were especially in view), the Greeks, and the Romans, while the birds stand for the prophetic movement among the Jews and the philosophy of those Greeks who 'became Christians before Christ'. Christ was to appear at a moment when not only was Israel purified but the other nations were also in some way prepared, at the end of the cycle of their own development. 'The East searches for the perfect God, the West for the perfect man, and *au fond* both feel the necessity of the opposed principle: the false man-god of the West, Caesar, and the mythical god-men of the East call out for the true God-man.'[33] Syncretistic Hellenism melded the two, Rome gave them political unity. But only Christianity could achieve the union of all. Israel prepared the natural bodiliness of the individual God-man, the pagan nations the social body of the collective God-man.

Solov'ëv's final chapter is devoted to the Messianic phase of the theocratic design: the term 'Kingdom of God' tends now to displace 'theocracy', just as 'Messiah' and 'Redeemer' have the edge on 'God-man', and, in a fashion faithful to the New Testament writings Solov'ëv insists on faith, hope and charity as well as such further virtues as meekness, humility, chastity and zeal that condition human participation in the Kingdom. 'Our internal disposition has to correspond with the external form of the Kingdom that has appeared in Christ.'[34] But the accentuated evangelicalism, spiritual and moral in tone, does not signal any abandonment of Solov'ëv's conviction of the all-encompassingness of the Messianic society.

So much for the fragmentary *History and Future of Theocracy*. The almost contemporaneous *La Russie et l'Église universelle*, written in French and published in Paris, arousing considerable 'proto-ecumenical' interest by its proposals, was surely Solov'ëv's best known writing in the contemporary West.[35] The Introduction attacks the limiting of the social action of Christianity to individual charity. Christendom cannot be deprived of the mission entailed in the 'royal' office of the Redeemer. 'The moral basis of the priestly union, or of the Church in the strict sense of the word, is faith and religious devotion; the kingly union of the Christian State is based on law and justice; while the element proper to the prophetic union or the perfect society is freedom and love.'[36]

> If the State, itself the product of human agencies and historic circumstances, is to bring mankind under the sway of absolute Justice, it must justify itself by submission to the Church which provides the moral and religious sanction and the actual basis for its work. It is equally clear that the perfect Christian society or the prophetic union, the reign of love and spiritual freedom, presupposes the priestly and kingly union. For the divine truth and grace cannot fully control the moral being of mankind nor effect its inner transformation unless they first have an objective force in the world, unless they are incarnate in a religious fact and upheld by law—unless, that is, they exist as Church and State.[37]

This claim does not mean that Solov'ëv had come to admire the Byzantine version of ecclesial-civil *symphonia*. After 842 (the ending of the iconoclast crisis), 'the Emperors permanently embraced "Orthodoxy" as an abstract dogma, while the orthodox prelates bestowed their benediction *in saecula saeculorum* on the paganism of Byzantine public life'.[38] He remained steadfastly anti-Byzantine, without, one would have thought, a sufficient grasp of the inner history of the East Roman polity to justify so unrelievedly hostile a stance.

Not that the experience of the West, whether mediaeval or modern, was much more encouraging.

> The two great historic experiments, that of the Middle Ages and that of modern times, seem to demonstrate conclusively that neither the Church lacking the assistance of a secular power which is distinct from but responsible to her, nor the secular State relying upon its own resources, can succeed in establishing Christian justice and peace on the earth. [Yet] the close alliance and organic union of the two powers *without confusion and without division* is the indispensable condition of true social progress.[39]

So Solov'ëv turns to the unique case of Russia.

> The profoundly religious and monarchic instinct of the Russian people, certain prophetic events in its past history, the enormous and compact bulk of its Empire, the great latent strength of the national spirit in contrast to the poverty and emptiness of its actual existence—all this seems to indicate that it is the historic destiny of Russia to provide the Universal Church with the political power which it requires for the salvation and regeneration of Europe and the world.[40]

Thus the Introduction ends.

In Part One of the *La Russie et l'Église universelle*, Solov'ëv considers the state of religion in Russia and the Christian East. His concern now is to identify what Russia needs so as to fulfil her theocratic mission. 'The distinctively religious character of the Russian people as well as the mystical tendency exhibited in our philosophy, our literature and our arts seem to indicate for Russia a great religious mission.'[41] The question is, What character does that mission have? The shift of gravity in Solov'ëv's preoccupations from philosophical to political concerns (in the widest sense of the latter) indicates the direction of an answer. Poignantly, given the sad events of 2018–19 when ecclesiastical Moscow and the throne of Constantinople parted company over the Church in Ukraine, Solov'ëv draws attention to the fragility of the outward structure of Orthodoxy.

> On the day on which the Russian and Greek Churches formally break with one another the whole world will see that the Oecumenical Eastern Church is a mere fiction and that there exists in the East nothing but isolated national Churches. That is the real motive which impels our hierarchy to adopt an attitude of caution and moderation towards the Greeks, in other words to avoid any kind of dealings with them.[42]

That strong suggestion of dissatisfaction with the outer shape of Orthodoxy is confirmed when he seeks to relate the question of

Church unity to the royal office of the Christian State. 'The State, if it is to be Christian, must be subject to the Church of Christ; but if this subjection is to be genuine, the Church must be independent of the State, it must possess a centre of unity outside and above the State, it must be in truth the Universal Church.'[43] But the 'centre of unity' needed cannot be found in East.

> First and foremost we must recognize ourselves for what we are in reality, an organic part of the great body of Christendom, and affirm our intimate solidarity with our Western brethren who possess the central organ which we lack. This moral act of justice and charity would be in itself an immense step forward on our part and the essential condition of all further advance.[44]

These claims advanced, Solov'ëv moves in Part Two of *La Russie et l'Église universelle* to consider the 'ecclesiastical monarchy founded by Jesus Christ'. If one admits in the Church the foundational power of the apostle Peter as the 'rock' of that edifice (for Solov'ëv, this was foretold in the schematic world-history of the Book of Daniel as well as recorded in the famous primacy text of St Matthew's Gospel, 16:18), it must exist somewhere—and there is only one serious candidate, the see of Rome. Wherever it may be it must at least be both international and independent and no other Christian see has this twofold character. Solov'ëv sets out his account of the Petrine office under the wider heading of the Church as temple of Christ, an ecclesiological key to Christendom as a 'sacerdotal union'.

But there is also of course the Church as body of Christ, which Solov'ëv now takes to be an ecclesiological key for Christendom as a 'royal union', englobing the nations and excluding only narrow nationalism. Here the 'members' of the 'body' of Christ will be the peoples, not individual persons. Byzantium had the mission to form a Christian empire and extend Christian truth to all social relations—but failed in its task, producing only a nominal version thereof. The East had successfully defined the divine humanity of Jesus at the Seven Councils. Yet the East did not know how best to draw out the consequences for the life of the Church or social life more generally. The Holy Roman (he calls it 'Franco-German') Empire, made a strenuous effort. Solov'ëv was thinking here of the Carolingian and Ottonian dynasties. But it was not enough. Under the Salians, that empire turned on the papacy which had appropriated the imperial role for itself, leading to the confusion for which Dante—avidly read by Solov'ëv in these years—sought a new emperor who would put an end to the commingling of the sacerdotal and royal powers.

As to the prophetic office: Solov'ëv, who had earlier considered the Reformation contribution a positive assistance to spiritual liberty, now implies the *munus propheticum* could never be assigned legitimately to Protestants. Egregiously, they failed to recognize adequately the other two offices, the *munus sacerdotale*, and the *munus regale*, and their study of the Bible had succumbed to hyper-criticism of the texts. While the prophetic office 'never receives systematic exposition in [Solov'ëv's] work', he appears to have considered it obvious that 'prophets of all times and ages ... are characterized precisely by a lack of definite characteristics: they are of all ages and genders, all classes and castes, all nations and traditions.'[45] They are not self-appointed, but neither are they without responsibility for their own condition. 'The infusion of divine grace received through prophetic freedom is conditional upon that "inner feat" [*podvig*] which allows such free activity to emerge.'[46] At least one prophet might be named—Solov'ëv himself, though he declined to propose the claim, conscious of the audacity involved. In *The History and Future of Theocracy* he had written, 'Prophets are principally bearers of theanthropic consciousness and representatives of the most profound moral union of the *whole* person and world with God—a union for whose sake the priesthood and monarchy exist.'[47]

But if he could hardly commend his own candidature for the *munus propheticum* he could at least suggest a suitable claimant to the *munus regale*. As Dmitri Strémooukhoff points out, Solov'ëv's highly personal interpretation of Russian history predisposed him to think his own nation best fitted to be the occupant of this office. Russia had already made two great 'sacrifices': firstly, the submission of the communal life of Kievan Rus' to the adjudication of Varangian rulers under the princes of the House of Rurik; secondly, Peter the Great's holocaust of Russian traditional *mores* in pupilage to the lessons of the European West. That suggests she is called to yield her own self-interest to a greater good, the reunion of Christendom and, thereby, the human family at large. Solov'ëv thought the presence of Jews and Poles within the Russian empire would help. The Jews know about the prophetic principle in biblical religion. The Poles are familiar with the sacerdotal principle through their attachment to the pope. Orthodox Russians are acutely aware of the royal principle since as the 'Third Rome' (a title Solov'ëv treats as more political than patriarchal or episcopal) they have inherited the imperial claims of Byzantium. Bringing about a free world-wide theocracy is the real mission of Russia. Solov'ëv took the artistic expression of the idea of Wisdom in the Novgorod School icons to hint at the 'social incarnation of Divinity in the universal Church.'[48]

In Part Three of *La Russie et l'Église universelle*, entitled, 'The Trinitarian Principle and its Social Application', Solov'ëv seeks to invoke Christian doctrine for his own constructions—bearing in mind his view that revelation cannot be a mystery accepted by faith alone, impenetrable to the reason of the members of the Church. It was at this point that Solov'ëv's Jesuit sponsors and promoters in Paris began to cover their ears, for in the context of late-nineteenth-century Latin Scholastic metaphysics and theology much of what he had to say could only seem wildly original—with the emphasis on the adverb rather than the noun. It is safe to say their Orthodox counterparts in Moscow and Petersburg would not have disagreed.

Once again (after two previous experiments in *The Philosophical Principles of Integral Knowledge* and the *Lectures on Godmanhood*), Solov'ëv attempts a proof of the Trinitarian dogma. He draws an inference from the fact that being must have a relation to essence, i.e. to its own determinate content, not least for God. To the absolute Being we must ascribe three constitutive modes of existence. It possesses its substance—its essence—in itself (absolute fact). It possesses that substance in its action which is necessarily the manifesting of this substance (absolute action). In the enjoyment of its being and action, it possesses the return to itself which proceeds from existence manifested by action (absolute enjoyment). One notable difference from the earlier proceedings is that the third Trinitarian hypostasis is now said to proceed from both the first and the second—implying Solov'ëv's acceptance, under Catholic influence, of some version of the *Filioque*, the contentious belief of Latin Christendom that the Spirit proceeds from the Father *and the Son*.

The 'essence' in question is 'uni-totality', and thus the Wisdom of God.[49] As Solov'ëv presents matters, the antithesis of divine being, chaos or 'bad infinity', is reduced by divine creative act to either nothingness or, at least, pure potentiality. But God must be more powerful than the realm of chaos not only in fact but also by right. And so to 'the pretensions of the infinitely manifold Chaos He must oppose not only His being pure and simple, but also a whole system of eternal ideas, reasons or truths, each one of which, linked with all the others by an indissoluble bond of logic, represents the triumph of determinate unity over anarchic plurality, over the Evil Infinity'.[50] 'The tendency of every particular being to assert itself exclusively as though it were the whole', a symptom of incipient return to chaos, is 'condemned as false and unjust by the system of eternal ideas which assigns to each a definite place in the absolute totality, thus displaying, alongside the truth of God, His justice and His equity'.[51] But the logical and ideal manifestation of its falseness is not the way to reduce it inwardly: that can only be done by 'a grace penetrating and transforming it and so drawing it back to unity'.[52] This explains the biblical 'rejoicing' of Wisdom (Proverbs 8:30). 'This rejoicing of Wisdom shews Him that all that is positive belongs to Him in fact and by right, that He possesses eternally in Himself an infinite treasure of all real powers, all true ideas, all gifts and all graces.'[53]

In a reprise of his Wisdom thinking in the *Lectures on Godmanhood*, Solov'ëv claims that God desires that there be outside him another nature which can become what he eternally is, the absolute whole. For this to occur, nature must be separated from God so as to be reunited to him in its summit, man. 'It is supremely in her vision of the earth and of Man that the eternal Wisdom unfolds her rejoicing before the God of the Future.'[54] But now there enters a fresh element when compared with the earlier presentation—a cosmology based on the notion of a *reversed transposition of the divine*. 'Unless we would repudiate the very notion of Godhead, we cannot admit outside of God any existence in itself, real and positive. What is outside God can therefore only be the Divine transposed or reversed. And this is what we primarily see in the [three] specific forms of finite existence that separate our world from God', three forms Solov'ëv identifies as extension, time, and mechanical causality. The 'extra-divine', considered as 'the divine transported or reversed', is produced under three relations. The divine uni-totality receives its reversed expression in extension where parts cannot penetrate each other. The coeternity of the divine hypostases has reversed expression in the form of time where each moment to enjoy actuality must exclude all others. The free relation of God to what-is-not-God finds reversed expression in the form of mechanical causality where the outward action of a given being is never the direct effect of its inward act.

These three laws which govern the creature imply an urge to fractionalize the body of the universe: 'an urge implies a will, and a will implies a psychical subject, that is to say, a soul'.[55] This deduction of the world soul is so framed as to lead into a re-assertion of its 'double and variable character'.[56] It can separate itself from God or attach itself to the divine Word, and so truly identify with (uncreated) Wisdom. To be able to do so, it must have an independent existence, and it is the desire for this existence which precipitates it into a chaotic state. Yet the world soul does not lose all aspiration toward unity, and by that draws to itself the action of the Word.

Solov'ëv clarifies the relation of the world soul to Wisdom by way of an exegetical study of Genesis 1:1 in the light of Proverbs 8.

> Divine Wisdom does not only represent the essential and actual uni-totality of the absolute being or substance of God, but also contains in itself the unifying principle of the divided and disintegrated being of the world. Being the accomplished

unity of the whole in God, it becomes also the unity of God and of existence outside the Godhead. It is thus the true rationale and end of Creation—the principle in which God created the heavens and the earth. While it exists substantially and from all eternity in God, it realizes itself effectively in the world and is successively incarnate therein, in drawing it back to an ever more perfect unity. At the beginning it is *reshith*, the pregnant notion of absolute unity, the unique principle which must unify all; at the end it is *malkhouth* (*basileia*, *regnum*), the Kingdom of God, the perfect and completely realized unity of the Creator and the creature.[57]

These observations indicate the continuing influence of the Kabbalah on Solov'ëv's mind. He stresses that Wisdom

is not the soul of the world; that is only the instrument, the medium and ground of its realization, which it approaches by the action of the Word and gradually raises itself to an ever more complete and real identification with itself. The soul of the world, considered in itself, is the indeterminate subject of Creation, equally accessible to the evil principle of Chaos and to the Word of God. The Chokmâh, Sophia, the Divine Wisdom, is not the soul, but the guardian angel of the world, overshadowing all creatures with its wings as a bird her little ones, in order to raise them gradually to true being.[58]

That would certainly explain a striking trait of the Novgorod icons. But Solov'ëv does nothing to bolster our confidence in his theological self-control when he adds, 'It is the substance of the Holy Spirit Who brooded over the dark waters of the forming world.'[59] A more satisfactory account of the relation of Wisdom to the Holy Spirit would have to await the later dogmatic writings of his principal theological heir, Father Sergeĭ Bulgakov.

The world as shaped by the soul of the world remains an ambiguous affair. The incarnation of Wisdom will have a long pregnancy. 'Thus the cosmic process is on the one hand the peaceful meeting, love and marriage of the two agents, the heavenly and the earthly, while on the other it is a mortal struggle between the Divine Word and the lower principle for the possession of the soul of the world.'[60] The soul of the world is the vehicle for the realization in the world of a Wisdom which at first is only possessed ideally by the creation, but at the end will be possessed really so in the integration of all (?) extra-divine existence with God. 'Natural humanity (Man, Woman and Society), as it emerges from the cosmic process, contains within itself only the possibility of such integration.'[61]

In any case, what transpired from Adam's Fall was human chaos. Only the operation of the Word could regenerate mankind. The Logos could make use in so doing of human temporality which, as past, present, and future has a kind of 'trinitarian form': 'the accomplished facts [preserved by the tradition of the past], the actions and tasks imposed by the needs of the present, and the aspirations towards a better state determined by a more or less perfect ideal of the future.'[62] As universal history moved forward the Word's activity bore fruit: in Mary as 'perfect Woman, or nature made divine'; in Jesus as 'perfect man or the God-Man', and in the Church—whose story, however, is still in process, the 'perfect society of God with men—the final incarnation of the eternal Wisdom.'[63] These three embodiments of Wisdom are held together not only sophianically but Christocentrically.

> Woman being only the complement of Man, and Society only his extension or total manifestation, there is fundamentally only a single divine-human being, the incarnate Sophia, whose central and completely personal manifestation is Jesus Christ, whose feminine complement is the Blessed Virgin, and whose universal extension is the Church.[64]

Thus 'Wisdom' can be applied to Christ, to Mary and, appealing to the Woman of the Apocalypse, to the Church—the latter, under the name of Holy Wisdom, venerated in Russian church dedications and icons.[65]

As truly as the divine Trinity possesses its essential Wisdom as its own 'substance', so truly does the Word incarnate 'in the trinity of His Messianic powers' possess his Spouse, the universal Church.[66]

The Theocratic Writings

To this Spouse-Body he delegates his messianic powers as priest, king, prophet, doing so according to a Trinitarian scheme, a *ratio Trinitatis*.[67] In a sophisticated discussion Solov'ëv explains.

> We know that in the Trinity absolute Unity is secured : (1) by the ontological primacy of the first hypostasis which is the original cause or principle of the two others, but not vice versa; (2) by the consubstantiality of all three, ensuring the indivisibility of their being; (3) by their perfect solidarity which does not permit of their acting separately. The social trinity of the Universal Church is the evolution of the ecclesiastical monarchy which contains in itself all the fullness of the messianic powers, unfolding itself in the three forms of Christian sovereignty. As in the Godhead, the unity of the Universal Church is secured: (1) by the absolute primacy of the first of these three powers, the pontificate, which is the only sovereignty directly and immediately instituted by God and therefore de jure the cause and necessary condition of the two others; (2) by the essential community of these three powers as included within the same Body of Christ and sharing the same substance of religion, the same faith, tradition and sacraments; (3) by the moral solidarity or community of aim which for all three can be nothing but the coming of the Kingdom of God, the perfect manifestation of the Universal Church.[68]

Having 'founded the Church upon His Priesthood and sanctioned the State by His Kingship, He has also provided for their unity and their unified progress by leaving to the world the free and living activity of His prophetic spirit'.[69] The unification of the human race on this basis is the realization of uni-totality in becoming.

How, then, is the Trinity doctrine applied socially? The 'Father' is represented by the priesthood (for communities by priests, for nations by bishops, for all humanity by the pope). But as the Father acts by the Son so the papacy acts by the Christian State, the second power. The third power, corresponding to the Holy Spirit, is needed so as to harmonize the others in view of the ideal future, hence the place of the prophet. 'What the priest begins by his mysterious rite, the secular prince must complete by legislation and the faithful people accomplish in its life.'[70] Solov'ëv sees the life of the faithful engaged in the seven sacraments, which he compares with seven pillars of Wisdom. Then 'the cycle of the sacraments, like the cycle of universal life, is completed by the resurrection of the flesh, the integration of the whole of humanity, the final incarnation of the divine Wisdom'.[71]

As already mentioned, Solov'ëv now spurned Slavophilism as ordered, nationalistically, to the greater glory of Russia, whereas Christian kenoticism requires an element of national renunciation, such as was shown in the request of the Kievan Rus' to the 'Varangians' to come and rule over them and Peter the Great's opening to the West which inevitably reduced the cultural autarchy of early Romanov Russia. (For Solov'ëv, Peter actually restored the spirit of Kievan Christianity, with its openness to Christendom at large.[72]) Now a third sacrifice was needed, if the 'Third Rome'—the seat of the tsar—is to reconcile the first two: the Constantinople of the Greek patriarchs and the Elder Rome of the popes. The 1854 dogmatization by Pope Pius IX of the eternally predestined Immaculate Conception of the Blessed Virgin Mary Solov'ëv felt to be a sort of approximation to the doctrine of Wisdom. Was there, then, a possibility that his sophianic doctrine could one day become the articulated faith of the Church? Solov'ëv had written positively about the notion of 'doctrinal development', explicitly in the context of reuniting the Catholic and Orthodox Churches: thus his essay 'The Development of Dogma in the Church in connection with the Question of Church Union', which appeared as a pamphlet in 1886.[73]

Until his last years—the time of the *Legend of Antichrist*—Solov'ëv continued to think of history as a developmental whole. In retrospect this irritated the premier historian of 'the ways of Russian theology', Georges Florovsky.

> One of the main tasks of the historian, according to Florovsky, is to uncover the immanent logic of metaphysical presuppositions and draw out the spiritual consequences

of any system of ideas. In this sense every historian should also be a philosopher—something which Florovsky was preeminently. But if we cannot detect a coherent pattern to the series of discrete individual, intellectual, and spiritual experiences, what is the point of studying them? The answer comes rather unexpectedly, though it has an old and distinguished ancestry: history is valuable for its exemplary function. It is the record of examples to be emulated or eschewed, the account of human frailty and error, as well as of spiritual victories that help man to be 'wiser for future times'.[74]

In point of fact Solov'ëv learned the hard way that history was not necessarily pointing in his direction.

Solov'ëv's debates in the ecclesiastical reviews about the possibility of Orthodox reconciliation with Catholicism, his correspondence and contacts with Catholic priests in Croatia (notably Bishop Josef Strossmayer at Djakovo) and in Paris, produced little result, though this flurry of ecumenical activity was not entirely ill-received: at least he was invited to lecture on the topic in the St Petersburg Ecclesiastical Academy. But his concept of a reunion of sister churches which, through osmosis, would produce a new reality—rather than a union by submission of the East to the Latin church as it stood, was well before its time. So it stubbornly remains.

NOTES

1. *Veliki spor i khristianskaya politika*, in Solov'ëv and Radlov, *Sobranie sochineniĭ*, IV, pp. 3–114. There is a translation into French, *La Grande Controverse et la politique chrétienne [Orient-Occident]* (Paris: Aubier, 1953).
2. *Ibid.*, p. 172.
3. *Ibid.*, p. 169. Italics original.
4. For Solov'ëv's attitude to the papal question, see Aidan Nichols, OP, 'Solovyov and the Papacy: A Catholic Evaluation', *Communio*, XXIV.1 (1997), pp. 143–59.
5. *La grande Controverse*, p. 177.

6. Cited by Strémoukhoff, *Vladimir Soloviev*, p. 134.
7. Wil van den Bercken, 'The Macrochristianity of Vladimir Solov'ëv. A Collectivist and Geographical Concept of Christian Religion', in van den Bercken, de Courten and van der Zweerde, *Vladimir Solov'ëv*, pp. 64–84, and here at, p. 76.
8. *Duchonii osnovi zhizni*, in Solov'ëv and Radlov, *Sobranie sochineniĭ*, III, pp. 299–416. The French translation, *Les Fondements spirituels de la vie* (Paris: Beauchesne, 1932), will be cited here, since the English equivalent *God, Man and the Church. The Spiritual Foundations of Life* (London: James Clarke, 1938), was made from the French not the Russian original.
9. *Ibid.*, p. 238.
10. *Ibid.*, p. 241.
11. *Ibid.*, p. 23.
12. *Ibid.*, p. 109.
13. *Ibid.*, pp. 135–6.
14. *Ibid.*, p. 144.
15. *Ibid.*, p. 148.
16. *Ibid.*, p. 150. Solov'ëv spells this out, naming each council, at p. 204.
17. *Ibid.*, p. 153.
18. Compare the following passage from the summary of Bulgakov's Christology printed as an appendix to his *Agnets Bozhiĭ* and the dependence on this section of the *Lectures on Godmanhood* leaps to the eye: 'The inhumanization of the Logos—with the acceptance of the measure of the human essence as the abandonment of the fullness of the Divine life and glory, "the descent from heaven"—is expressed in the fact that, for him, the limit of the human is also His own limit', *The Lamb of God*, p. 445.
19. *Les Fondements spirituels de la vie*, p. 154.
20. *Ibid.*, p. 158.
21. *Ibid.*, p. 159.
22. *Ibid.*, pp. 163–4, 170.
23. *Ibid.*, p. 171.
24. *Ibid.*, p. 174.
25. *Ibid.*, p. 213.
26. *Ibid.*, p. 226.
27. *Istoriya i budushchnost' teokratii*, in Solov'ëv and Radlov, *Sobranie sochineniĭ*, IV, pp 241–633.
28. Cited in Strémoukhoff, *Vladimir Soloviev*, p. 144.

29. *Ibid.*, p. 145.
30. *Ibid.*, p. 145–6, 146.
31. *Istoriya i budushchnost' teokratii*, in Solov'ëv and Radlov, *Sobranie sochineniĭ*, IV, p. 258.
32. *Ibid.*, pp. 254, 256.
33. Strémooukhoff, *Vladimir Soloviev*, p. 156.
34. van den Bercken, 'The Macrochristianity of Vladimir Solov'ëv', p. 82.
35. *La Russie et l'Église universelle* (Paris: Albert Savine, 1889); the English translation is *Russia and the Universal Church* (London: Geoffrey Bles, 1948).
36. *Ibid.*, p. 9.
37. *Ibid.*, p. 11.
38. *Ibid.*, pp. 24–5.
39. *Ibid.*, p. 31. Italics original.
40. *Ibid.*
41. *Ibid.*, p. 46.
42. *Ibid.*, pp. 69–70.
43. *Ibid.*, p. 77.
44. *Ibid.*, p. 81.
45. Smith, *Vladimir Soloviev and the Spiritualization of Matter*, p. 200.
46. *Ibid.*, p. 201.
47. Cited *ibid.*, p. 202.
48. Strémooukhoff, *Vladimir Soloviev*, p. 176.
49. *Ibid.*, pp. 156–7.
50. *Ibid.*, p. 158.
51. *Ibid.*
52. *Ibid.*
53. *Ibid.*, p. 160.
54. *Ibid.*
55. *Ibid.*, p. 162.
56. *Ibid.*
57. *Ibid.*, pp. 166–7.
58. *Ibid.*, p. 167.
59. *Ibid.*
60. *Ibid.*, p. 171.

61. *Ibid.*, p. 175.
62. *Ibid.*, p. 181.
63. *Ibid.*, p. 175.
64. *Ibid.*, p. 176.
65. *Ibid.*, p. 177.
66. *Ibid.*, p. 195.
67. *Ibid.*, p. 196.
68. *Ibid.*
69. *Ibid.*, p. 206.
70. Cited by Strémooukhoff, *Vladimir Soloviev*, p. 186.
71. *Russia and the Universal Church*, p. 214.
72. Pauline Schrooyen, 'Vladimir Solov'ëv: Critic or Heir of Slavophilism?', in Deutsch Kornblatt and Gustafson, *Russian Religious Thought*, pp. 13–27, especially p. 18.
73. 'Dogmaticheskoe razvitie tserkvÿ v svyazi s voprosom o soedinenii tserkveï', in Solov'ëv and Radlov, *Sobranie sochineniĭ*, IX (supplementary volume), pp. 1–67. There is a careful discussion of its ecumenical significance in Valliere, *Modern Orthodox Theology*, pp. 178–92.
74. Raeff, 'Enticements and Rifts', pp. 277, 278.

☩ 4 ☩

A NEW START
AND THE FINAL COMING

After 1881, Solov'ëv's life in Russia was often hard. His income was small, though his friends competed to host him. He had broken with the Slavophiles, his natural allies, and was obliged to write for Liberal papers.

> Spiritually and emotionally, Solov'ëv was isolated, and—partly through the ecclesiastical censors—he was effectively cut off from many of his previous allegiances and natural-seeming allies. Solov'ëv felt this very strongly indeed: this can be judged in the correspondence of the time, in which he cites Mikhail Lermontov's bitter poem *Blagodarnost'* [Gratitude], which gives thanks for "the vengeance of enemies and the slander of friends".[1]

His tone towards the Slavophiles became irritable, even angry. Thus in *The National Question in Russia* (articles from 1883 to 1891 collected as a book) he claimed that Slavophile 'orthodoxism' (*pravoslavnichanie*) was more a faith in the Russian people themselves than in that people's Orthodox faith. Khomyakov's eulogy of Orthodox unity-plus-freedom had been hopelessly abstract. The Slavophile view that the Russian people had confided governmental care to the autocracy was equally idealistic. And in any case, the Slavophile ideals were not uniquely Russian or even Slav. They could be found in Western Catholic writers, such as in Hugues Félicité Robert de Lamennais, who espoused a form of theocratic democracy (but eventually abjured Christianity), and the (somewhat more promising) figure of the Tübingen theologian Johann Adam Moehler, whose theology of the Church community emphasized the role of the Holy Spirit in bringing about its unity. It must be said that these parallels with classical Slavophilism are not especially close. But they served Solov'ëv's polemical purpose.

Solov'ëv had come to believe himself more orthodox than the Orthodox Church in the East since, unlike that Church, he admitted what he took to be a universal early tradition about the primatial chair of Peter at Rome. Yet fearing papal disapproval he failed to present himself in April 1888 for the audience with Leo XIII Bishop Strossmayer had arranged for him. The Jesuits with whom he corresponded began to realize how far removed his plans for reunion were from any schemes they might entertain, while the metaphysics of the theosophical sections of *La Russie et l'Église universelle* struck them as altogether alien. Strossmayer alone remained faithful, as witness his 1888 telegram to Kiev for the Baptism of Rus'. Written in the spirit of Solov'ëv's project, it displeased Pope Leo. Strossmayer's own star was fading. It was at this time that he retired from Croatian public life after a public rebuke from the Austro-Hungarian emperor, Franz Joseph, for apparently preferring Russia to Hungary (the Ban or governor of Croatia was responsible, under the terms of the 1867 *Ausgleich* which created the 'Dual Monarchy' not to Vienna but to Budapest). Plainly, Solov'ëv was in danger of being shunned by both sides. Towards 1891 he was advised by fellow-Orthodox henceforth to confess to Catholic priests. On what would become a celebrated occasion in 1896, he received Communion from the hands of a Uniate priest, formerly Orthodox, Father Nicholas Tolstoy, who had a private oratory in his apartment. It was the feast of Pope St Leo I, to whom, apparently, Solov'ëv felt a great attachment. Though he prepared for the act of communicating by reading out the (so-called) Creed of the Council of Trent, it is going too far to say that he saw this as 'a secret union with the Catholic Church'—which is how Sergeĭ Solov'ëv presents the matter in his biography.[2] (Sergeĭ became, clandestinely, a priest of the Russian Catholic Exarchate during its brief period of active existence in Russia between the

February Revolution and the advent of Bolshevik persecution.[3] The temptation to make his uncle the Exarchate's patron *avant la lettre* was evidently too great—and the 'patronage' is not altogether undeserved.) Vladimir Solov'ëv would not communicate again until an Orthodox priest came to his death-bed.

He began to worry obsessively about the Yellow Peril, the future expansion of the Far Eastern powers. Russia's defeat by Japan five years after his death gave credence to his anxieties. Meanwhile, in the great famine of 1891–2—it started on the Volga but spread to the Urals and the Black Sea, and caused up to several hundred thousand deaths—he noted with immense sadness that while the imperial government had done something to alleviate distress, civil society in Russia contributed almost nothing. Meanwhile, throughout Europe, Nietzscheanism—a philosophy of the will-to-power he feared and hated—was spreading.[4]

Rebuffed in his hopes for the corporate life of the churches—and of Russia—he turned now to new means: specifically, to a Liberal Christian politics, and to 'theurgy'. In his essays 'On the decadence of the mediaeval conception of the world' and 'À propos falsifications' he set out to appeal to Liberals. Surely they should sympathize with a preparation of the Kingdom of God by the gradual practical amelioration of human affairs? And he started to write on new subjects: beauty in nature and art, and human love. These last writings on beauty and the meaning of love (along with his life of Plato) consider the aesthetic activity which previously he had liked to call 'theurgic'. Their beauties are the beginning of the incarnation of Wisdom in the sensuous. In an encyclopaedia article on mysticism, Solov'ëv included an account of the 'active mysticism' of which theurgy might be said to form part.[5] Perfect art is, he thought, creative mysticism, while in physical nature the soul-of-the-world is already in flight towards God. The beauty of nature is an incipient incarnation of the Wisdom that art pursues. Material existence cannot be introduced into the moral order unless it is spiritualized—introduced into the form of beauty—through (in Strémooukhoff's words) 'the transfiguration of matter by the incarnation in it of another supra-material principle', the principle of Wisdom.[6] If we ask, how Solov'ëv understood such transfiguration, the answer coheres with his wider *Weltanschauung*: it is an anticipatory realization of the positive uni-totality of the consummated divine plan, or in Strémooukhoff's summary, a 'sensuous representation of some object in the light of the future world'.[7] The 'spiritualization of matter' has as its goal nothing less than the coming of the Kingdom of God: 'the full definition and penetration of the material principle by the spirit and, conversely, the full habitation of spirit in material form'.[8]

As to *The Meaning of Love*, *Smÿsl lyubvi* (a book originally serialized in the journal *Voprosÿ filosofii i psikhologii* in the years 1892–4): whereas the nuptials of the New Adam and the New Eve took place at the Incarnation, their union needs to be reflected in multiple paired hypostases by a marital practice that restores the androgyne, the image of God in male and female *together* in an intimately unified life. (Solov'ëv was anticipated in this belief by Baader, whose writings enjoyed a certain celebrity in religiously-minded circles in Russia during the reign of Alexander I.) The love of a husband must be at once both for an earthly wife and also for the Eternal Feminine—'which is not merely an inert image in the Divine mind, but a living spiritual essence possessed of all the fullness of power and activity'.[9] Woman is its ('her') living icon—the 'element of adoration and boundless devotion, which, though peculiar to love, yet possesses so little meaning, if it refers only to the earthly object of it, in separation from the heavenly one'.[10] Plato had not been far wrong when he sought in love, *eros*, the link between mortal life and the realm of the everlasting Ideas.

There is a parallel between Solov'ëv's approach to conjugal love with that of the Anglo-Catholic lay theologian Charles Williams who would have preferred, however, the adjective 'romantic'. That is so even if two clear differences distinguish these thinkers where the category of 'lovers' is concerned. In *The Meaning of Love* Solov'ëv thinks only of conjugal love, and takes his account to be the benchmark for all authentic married love. Williams thinks adoring love can exist outside of married state with its sexual relations. That, after all, was true of Dante's experience of Beatrice, and the case of Dante was crucial for Williams' emerging 'romantic' theology. Though a wide-ranging if sketchy *Outlines of Romantic Theology*—written 1924, published posthumously—was probably inspired chiefly by Coventry Patmore's poetry, Dante's *Commedia* and Malory's *Morte d'Arthur* were not far behind,[11] while Williams' re-reading of the former in the course of the 1930s made possible the fully Dantesque 'The Theology of Romantic Love'—chapter 5 of *He Came Down from Heaven*—in 1938,[12] and the essay-length *Religion and Love in Dante: the Theology of Romantic Love* in 1941,[13] as well as the fully-fledged *The Figure of Beatrice. A Study in Dante* in 1944.[14] Also unlike Solov'ëv, Williams thought there can be true marriages without an 'adoring love' with explicitly or implicitly transcendental implications. Speaking of the married, he writes: The "falling in love" often happens, but it is not to be either demanded or denied. There are many modulations and combinations of vision, affection, and appetite, and none of these modulations is necessarily an improper beginning for that great experiment which we call marriage.'[15]

In Solov'ëv's own biography, there is not only the Beatrician experience of the boy, but also the (seemingly sexually unconsummated) devotion to the 'Madonna of the Steppes' of the grown man—both of which, as it happens, fit better with Williams' template than with Solov'ëv's own. Moreover, Solov'ëv's treatise on love would not have been so readily dismissed as an unrealistic picture of the matrimonial condition if, like Williams, he had admitted the existence of other modes in which the physical and social elements of the married life are brought together. Williams was judicious when he declared, 'The clearest possibility of this Way, and perhaps the most difficult, may be in marriage, but the suggestion of it is defined wherever the suggestion of adoration is present'.[16]

Williams could make the claim for a link between the beloved and the Eternal without recourse to a postulated feminine essence in the divine realm.

> What Dante sees is the glory of Beatrice as she is in 'heaven'— that is, as God chose her, unfallen, original; or (if better)

redeemed; but at least, either way, celestial. What he sees is something real. It is not 'realer' than the actual Beatrice who, no doubt, had many serious faults, but it is as real. Both Beatrices are aspects of one Beatrice. The revealed virtues are real; so is the celestial beauty.[17]

That is not to say, however, that Williams's account, with its focus on the Dante-Beatrice relation, is without a wider speculative theological intent. In Williams' interpretation of the 'pageant scene' in the last Canto of the *Purgatorio*, when the Dante character is 'brought right up to where Beatrice and the Griffin face each other', he 'sees her "shining eyes" gazing into the eyes of the Griffin'—the mythical beast representing Christ as the 'twy-natured' God-man; at that point the Dante character 'sees the double nature mirrored in hers',[18] and thus the 'unity' of the Word incarnate in the reciprocally existing 'exchanged two Natures'.[19] Specifically, he sees it as reflected in the twofold modality of Beatrice's own being as a fallen yet glorified creature. There is *some* affinity here to Solov'ëv's notion of the active unity of the Logos reflected in the passive unity of Sophia—of which created Wisdom, in its ambivalent condition in a post-lapsarian world still in process of salvation, is the finite expression. That is pertinent to the last meeting of Dante and Beatrice in canto XXXI of the *Paradiso*, where he implores her, 'Guard your magnificence in me, that my soul, which you have made whole, may please you when it unknots itself from the body'. He adds, 'I prayed thus, and she, so far away as she seemed, smiled and gazed; then she turned herself to the eternal fountain', namely, the divine Trinity.[20]

In Solov'ëv's anthropology in *The Meaning of Love*, such love is closely connected with truth, since it rescues man from 'false self-assertion'.[21] Love rectifies individuality through 'the sacrifice of egoism'.[22] Conjugal love is the fullest expression of this sacrifice, which is why popular usage is justified in treating as synonymous love at large and conjugal (or potentially conjugal) love in particular. 'Not in vain is it that sexual relations are not merely termed love, but that, by general acknowledgement, also they represent love *par excellence*, exhibiting the type and ideal of all other kinds of love (cf. the Song of Songs and the Apocalypse).'[23] As Solov'ëv explains, 'In all other kinds of love there is lacking either homogeneity, equality and reciprocity between the lover and the loved one, or the all-round diversity of those who are to complete the characters of each other'.[24] This is not simply a question of empirical psychology. It is a matter of entering upon the fullness of ideal personality—which itself can be distinguished only conceptually from the image of God when fully achieved. 'The authentic man in the fullness of his ideal personality, obviously, cannot be merely male or merely female, but must be the supreme unity of both.'[25] For this to amount to the realization of divine imagehood, there must be included, however, the most strenuous moral and spiritual programme.

> For the beginning passive receptivity of feeling suffices, but subsequently active faith is indispensable, with moral exertions and toil to keep for oneself, to strengthen and unfold this gift of luminous and creative love, in order by means of it to incarnate in oneself and in another the image of God, and out of two finite and perishable natures to create one absolute and immortal individuality. If, inevitably and without our own volition, the existent idealization of love reveals to us, through what is empirical and visible, a far-off ideal image of the beloved object, this is not of course, that we might only delight in it, but that in the strength of true faith, of active imagination and real creativeness, we might transform, in accordance with this authentic exemplar, whatever does not actually correspond to it, and must embody it in a real phenomenon.[26]

The physical aspect of sex, like the social dimension of marriage, finds its proper place only when the primacy of this high spiritual aspiration is acknowledged.[27]

Did Solov'ëv intend to imply that only such couples can be in the divine image? Such an inference might be drawn from *The Meaning of Love* but it is hardly compatible with the Church's calendar of saints. Certainly he maintains there can be no fuller union with

God than the one offered via this route.

> In sex-love, truly understood and truly realized in bodily act, this Divine essence [the Eternal Feminine] receives the means for its definitive and ultimate incarnation in the individual life of man, the mode of the deepest and at the same time the most outward and actually perceptible union with it, [hence] those beams of an unearthly felicity, of a gladness not of this world, by which love even when imperfect is accompanied.[28]

If his treatise is deafeningly silent on the topic of offspring this is presumably because he included their procreation and nurture under the heading of love's social dimension—though this scarcely does justice to the way husband and wife can re-discover each other in and through their children.

These weaknesses are compensated in part by Solov'ëv's subtly elaborated account of the analogical relation which holds good between God/Christ/the husband, on the one hand, and, on the other, the world/the Church/the wife.[29] The second and third of these pairings are familiar enough from the Letter to the Ephesians (5:22–32), but Solov'ëv takes nuptiality further back, historically and ontologically, into the depths of the (ideal) relation of God and the world. Like all analogies, the symmetry that holds good among these three pairings has its limits, as Solov'ëv himself recognized.

> God receives nothing from the creature for Himself, i.e. no kind of augmentation, but gives everything to it. Christ receives from the Church no increase at all in the sense of perfection, and gives all perfection to her, but He does receive from the Church increase in the sense of the fullness of his collective body. Finally, man and his female alter ego mutually complete each other, not only in the real but also in the ideal sense, attaining perfection only through action upon one another.[30]

All this is deftly worked out, but in his enthusiasm for the marital analogy Solov'ëv reverses the order whereby the monastic life trumps the life of marriage as a Christian calling. True marriage is positive asceticism, monasticism its negative counterpart. The latter may lead to *angellosis*, becoming like the angels, but the former can lead to *theosis*, becoming like God.

1896 was the year of his controversial act of auricular confession to a Catholic priest, recital of the Creed of Trent, and communion in the Eucharistic sacrament. Solov'ëv, unlike the priest who ministered to him, did not see this as a disavowal of Orthodoxy, but as a foretaste of the union to come. 'To come'—but how and when? He was now preoccupied with a preliminary coming, the advent of the Antichrist. The questions that exercised him were, firstly, how to prepare people for making the choice for or against Christ and, secondly, what collaboration in divine-humanity could mean if the end of all things was actually to be entirely preternatural—to supervene in a way unprepared by any achieved spiritual progress on society's part. Solov'ëv's pastoral compassion lies behind the first question, and an understandable unwillingness to jettison the whole of his previous work (whether on theosophy, theocracy, or theurgy) the second. This problematic dominates the 1898 *Three Conversations*. But it is already found in the preface to his last major philosophical writing, *The Justification of the Good*.

The writing of *The Justification of the Good* was from a methodological point of view something of a new beginning. From an autobiographical perspective, however, its subject-matter was altogether fitting to one whose life-work was drawing to its close. In the preface to its second edition, from 1899, the year preceding his death, Solov'ëv gave as his aim to show how the good is the truth—meaning, as he writes, 'the one correct path that is true to itself and is to be followed on all occasions in life and to the end.'[31] According to its most recent English translator, this substantial work 'remains even today the simple most comprehensive and systematic ethical treatise in the Russian language.'[32] It 'was to be not just a theoretical treatise, but a manual, outlining, albeit only in broad strokes, how to achieve the meaning of life, which lies in connecting our individual and social being with the "Perfect Moral Good"—one of Solov'ëv's various locutions for the Deity.'[33]

Dmitri Strémooukhoff spoke in this connection of the 'new reconstruction' of Solov'ëv's thought,[34] and certainly there is innovation when, in the Introduction, he tells readers that moral philosophy is by no means entirely dependent on religious and metaphysical principles. Epistemology, at any rate, is *de trop* since, as Thomas Nemeth explains, in this work 'Solov'ëv held that the object of ethics is of our own creation, namely, our actions and thoughts, which are certainly known to us, and therefore there is no need in advance in an ethical study to inquire how we know the external world and the limits of that presumed knowledge.'[35] Still, Solov'ëv was not proposing to sunder ethics from other disciplines that seek truth—and find it. That the will to know the truth for truth's sake is 'approved by our moral conscience ... demonstrates the profound unity of Goodness and Truth.'[36] Fragmentary beginnings of a treatise on 'Theoretical Philosophy', begun in the year *The Justification of the Good* was finished, took philosophical thought to be 'the conscientious search, pressed to its conclusion, of truth proved with certitude.'[37] The torso of the work has suggested to some an anticipation of the phenomenology of Edmund Husserl, or the related ontological enquiries of Alexius Meinong: psychology must give way to sheer intentionality, the centre of epistemic attention be displaced from the 'I', psychologically considered, to the object, or, better, to the truth sought.[38]

With *The Justification of the Good* there is, fortunately, no need for second guessing how Solov'ëv would continue his work. The treatise is both well-structured and complete.[39] Although the concept of the good is in the possession of all human beings, Solov'ëv is concerned with those who have set out to follow it—even if the complete justification of the good in its fullness can be made known to all minds only when Jesus Christ is recognized not just as the absolute principle of the good but as its fullness. Meanwhile the good can still be justified theoretically, and the way of righteousness sketched out for those who have made a choice to walk thus. In this respect, Strémooukhoff compares *The Justification of the Good* to the *Philokalia*, the monumental Byzantine-Slav anthology of ascetical and mystical teaching, for in each case the aim is divinization.⁴⁰ Solov'ëv's new book remained, however, resolutely philosophical—not theological—in idiom. Whereas Kant set himself to grasp the purity of the good, in its freedom from empirical calculation, Solov'ëv aimed to bring out its fullness, its uni-totality—which meant, in Strémooukhoff's words, 'to present the totality of moral norms in the entire realm of individual and collective life'.⁴¹

The book falls into three parts which consider in turn the good in human nature, the good as coming from God, and the good as developing in human history. In a survey of the 'original data of morality' (chapter 1), Solov'ëv considers some basic traits of man's nature, when contrasted with the animal kingdom. *Shame*, which belongs with human sexuality, allows man to affirm moral dignity: spirit should not be enslaved to matter. Ethics will entail a struggle for the independence of the spirit, on which the ascetic masters could instruct us (chapter 2). The other basic springs of morals for Solov'ëv are pity or sympathy (as in his earlier, Schopenhauer-influenced ethics) and piety (also translated 'reverence' or 'respect'). *Pity* recognizes the bond which binds all beings together. It is the foundation of altruism (chapter 3). *Piety*, initially towards parents and then, by extension and transference, towards the will of the Father, is the basis for all religion, and furnishes morals with its stress on the objective autonomy of the good, lending its sanction to moral commands (chapter 4). When the theological virtues of faith and hope are considered in a moral perspective, then they coincide with piety. The last of the theological virtues, charity, finds expression in the living out of three moral maxims which are all-important for Solov'ëv's scheme. Do not love the world. Love God with all your heart. Love your neighbour as yourself.⁴² This trio of commands embraces relation to the lower, relation to the higher, and relation to the equal. Asceticism (compare shame), altruism (compare pity) and religion (compare reverence) are thus the three most foundational attitudes of the moral life, but none must be adopted to the exclusion of the rest any more than there can be picking and choosing among the three governing maxims.

Solov'ëv rules out in advance any merely 'psychologistic' understanding of his doctrine—thus, perhaps, ratifying in advance the suggestion recorded above that he now walked a parallel path to the early phenomenologists. As he writes at the close of his chapter on the virtues (chapter 5): 'Although these norms *rest psychologically* on the respective primary feelings of shame, pity and reverence, these norms do not have their ultimate factual foundation in these feelings, but are developed logically from the idea of *what should be*, or *truth* (in the broad sense).'[43] And he goes on to characterize such truth in terms of the three maxims.

> Such truth, moral truth, demands that we treat our lower nature as lower, i.e. that we subordinate it to our rational goals. If, on the contrary, we subordinate ourselves to our lower nature, we recognize it not as it is, in fact, but as something higher. In other words, we distort the true order of things. We violate the moral truth and treat this lower sphere improperly, i.e., immorally. In the same way, moral truth demands that we treat those similar to ourselves in the same fashion, namely, that we recognize their equality with us, that we place ourselves in their shoes. If, in recognizing ourselves as individuals with equal right, we see others only as empty masks, then obviously we step back from the truth and our relationship is not what it should be. Finally, if we are aware of a higher universal principle than ourselves, then more truth demands that we treat it as higher, i.e., with religious respect. Any other attitude would contradict the true order of things, and, consequently, would not be as it should.[44]

The question that immediately arises is how awareness of moral truth (i.e. of proper relation to everything, inferior, equal, or superior) comes to enjoy such power for human life. In Solov'ëv's words, this is a 'new task of reason', namely, 'to find a practical principle that is not only something that should be, but is also something *desirable* to the highest degree both in itself and for everyone. It would have of its essence the power to determine human behavior with necessity, independently both of the natural inclinations of the soul and of the degree of one's spiritual development—a principle that all people equally have and is understandable to and real for everyone.'[45] The question before him is an ancient one. What is for human beings the *summum bonum*?

In seeking the fundamental moral principle, with the attributes of necessity and universality that must belong to it, Solov'ëv rejects in turn hedonistic eudaimonism, autarchy, and utilitarianism, all of them regarded as 'abstract eudaimonism in its various forms' or 'pseudo-principles of practical philosophy' (chapter 6), before proceeding to his own answer in part two of *The Justification of the Good*.

The need to discuss the good 'of' or 'from' God arises in this context from the disparity between the desire for happiness and the reasonable duty to be virtuous. Solov'ëv is obliged to confront the challenge of Kantian formalism in ethics, for Kant was also preoccupied with this very issue (chapter 7). Solov'ëv's solution will also seek to harmonize an ethics of duty with an ethics of happiness but in a more radically (directly) theistic way. 'If man chooses the way of integrity, he directs himself toward immortality, if he has pity on his fellows, he wishes to acquire immortality for everyone. The Good thus becomes the means to arrive at beatitude, which must satisfy man. So the morals of pure duty is reconciled with that of eudaimonism.'[46] If genuine *eudaemonia* is 'determined by the moral good' then there can be 'no contradiction between the ethics of pure duty and eudaemonism in general.'[47] The reconciliation of the two will come about via the acknowledgement in one's life of the religious principle which takes the ultimate object of reverence and the supreme moral good to be one and the same (chapter 8). It pertains to piety, of the three sets of 'primordial data' in the moral life, to find imperfection in ourselves, perfection in God, and the reconciliation of the two 'in a process of becoming perfect (or the process whereby the first comes to agree with the second)', which is indeed, for Solov'ëv 'our life's task.'[48] Compare the *Philokalia*—and of course Solov'ëv's version of the categorical imperative, 'Be perfect!', is a citation from the Scriptures.[49] Anticipating the 'full scope of our definitive assimilation [to] and unification with the Deity', we 'already have a foretaste of the joy of this fulfilment'.[50]

That perfecting will not be confined to individual living; it will also contribute to the general perfecting of the social mass. That is not so obviously a concern of the Philokalic tradition, but at Solov'ëv's hands it is no retreat into humanitarianism but an orientation of self to the eschatological Church. The perfecting of society entails not only moral perfection but immortality. 'Perfection' denotes 'the unity of the moral good and the real good',[51] in view of the definitive revelation of the Kingdom in the world. 'The entire historical process produces the real conditions under which the moral good can actually become common property and without which it cannot be realized,'[52] in a 'long and difficult transition from bestial humanity to divine humanity'.[53] Chapter 10 is concerned with the impossibility of setting the individual against humanity.

By that chapter Solov'ëv has identified the place of Christ as central and indispensable. When discussing the 'reality of the moral order' (chapter 9), Solov'ëv remarks that 'the human spirit has proceeded to the *idea* of the Kingdom of God and the *ideal* of the divine person along two paths: Jewish prophetic inspiration and Greek philosophical thought'.[54] Yet 'this idea in its essence cannot remain abstract or purely speculative; it demands *incarnation*'.[55] 'A human god, even though in the form of a universal sovereign, is an empty illusion, whereas the divine human being can reveal his reality in the form of a wandering rabbi'.[56] The Kingdom of God is not to be understood as simply the outcome of the development of the human world. When Christ, the true God-man appeared, it was as 'the first and central manifestation of the Kingdom of God which is the absolute moral order and the resurrection of all. Founder of a new Kingdom towards which the preceding realm, that of natural humanity, tended without being able to reach it, Christ opens to the latter the doors of the Kingdom of God'.[57] But the revelation of the Kingdom is not as yet its full realization which cannot be had without the engagement of human freedom in ascetic, altruistic, and religious action (compare shame, pity, piety). The difference made by Christ—the manifestation of the Kingdom in his life, death, resurrection and the sending of the Spirit—is that the integral humanity of the future will be the fullness of all the positive particularities of the new or regenerated creation, englobing the old but not confined to it.

In describing the 'principal eras in the development of personal-social consciousness' (chapter 11), Solov'ëv finds he cannot prescind from theological comment on the historical periodization. 'Without going into the metaphysical aspect of Christian belief, I simply have in mind here the fact that Christianity (and it alone) is built upon the idea of the actually perfect person and the perfect society. Consequently, it promises to fulfil the demand for a true infinity that we have in our human consciousness.'[58] The ideal cosmos of Platonism is only a 'semi-universalism'; it represents only the 'conceivable' side of things. 'Only the absolute principle embodied in the Sun of righteousness penetrates into the depths of earthly reality, creates a new life in it and is realized as a new order of being—as the all-united Kingdom of God.'[59]

In chapters 12 and 13 Solov'ëv reiterates the inseparability of individual and social, and in five succeeding chapters (14 to 18), considers the implications for the nation, for punishment, for economics, for law (the coercive demand for the realization of a certain minimum of the Good), and for war, before a final chapter on the 'moral organization of humanity as a whole'. Family, nation, and (global) humanity are the crucial strata, for we 'must understand and accept the positive elements of life in their relative and temporary manifestations as *conditional data for the solution of an unconditional task*.'[60] 'Family' is an opportunity for him to rehearse the peculiar view of marriage found in *The Meaning of Love*; as to 'nation', among the three factors of physical descent, language and history, Solov'ëv finds the second by far the most important (the first is largely fictitious and the third cannot be understood without invoking general history); 'humanity' gives us the 'final subject' of the moral organization of man, though this is humanity with its component parts—nations, families, individuals. It is an opening for Solov'ëv to reiterate once again his ecclesiology, for 'The catholicity of the church is the fundamental form of the moral organization of humanity and is the conscious and deliberate solidarity of all the members of the universal body for the single unconditional goal of existence coupled with a full "division of spiritual labor", of gifts and services, which express and realize the goal."[61] This is not said so as to eliminate the need for the State. 'Christianity demands of us not that we reject or limit the sovereignty of the State, but that we fully recognize the principle that can give the state its real, complete meaning, namely, its moral solidarity with the concern of the Kingdom of God on earth, with the intrinsic subordination of all secular goals to the one Spirit of Christ'.[62] Society considered as an economic union means for Solov'ëv the collective organization of our attitude to lower nature, including our own. Here Solov'ëv recommends an attitude of abstinence, aimed at the full possession of physical nature by 'nurtur[ing] it in love'.[63] In his conclusion, Solov'ëv speaks of what he has described as a triadic love: ascending love towards absolute perfection, God, equalization of love towards all those who can share it, other humans, and descending love towards material nature insofar as the latter can be brought within the scope of absolute love. The systematic nature of *The Justification of the Good* appears when we realize that the investigation has come full circle, and returned to the primordial data of human nature from which Solov'ëv set out, shame, pity, piety. The forms of moral organization are the universal Church as piety organized collectively, the State which is organized pity, and economic society which has as specific principle the abstinence that flows from shame (abstinence from carnal excess in view of the transfiguration of matter). The conclusion looks ahead to the unfinished 'Theoretical Philosophy': having considered the good qua good in moral philosophy, it must now be considered as truth in epistemology and metaphysics. But for Solov'ëv time was running out.

In *Three Conversations*, from 1898 to 1899, a motley gathering of figures—a society hostess, a retired general, a senior civil servant, a Tolstoyan aristocrat and Solov'ëv himself—discuss in animated fashion war, morality and religion.[64] The last conversation brings them soon enough to the theme of the Antichrist, on which topic a narrative of a possible ultimate future scenario is read out (fictively: the work of a recently deceased monk). The dialogue form was influenced by the fact that he had just finished translating Platonic dialogues, but his French translator Eugène Tavernier thought the style too reminiscent of Joseph de Maistre's *Soirées de Saint-Pétersbourg* for this to be mere coincidence.[65] For his part Balthasar calls Solov'ëv's last preoccupation, with Apocalypse and Antichrist, a 'salutary counterpoise to his evolutionism, a counterpoise lacking in Teilhard [the twentieth-century Jesuit cosmologist] right up to the end'.[66]

A spring visit to Egypt in 1898 had reminded him of the disappointment of hopes Egypt had once inspired. He told friends he had seen devils.[67] The contemporary world lay under the dominion of economic materialism, abstract moralism, and the demonism of the Superman (i.e. governed by Marx, Tolstoy and Nietzsche). More especially, Solov'ëv's fear (not without earlier premonitions) was that the truth, goodness and beauty he had sought and celebrated could be 'so-opted into the service of a corrupted ideal'.[68]

Solov'ëv's concept of the Antichrist, so Strémoukhoff points out, is not unlike that of the fifth-century bishop Cyril of Jerusalem's in the fifteenth of Cyril's *Mystagogical Catecheses*. The Antichrist appears to solve all problems. In Solov'ëv's 'Legend' (or 'Short Story'), 'the genial book of the Antichrist, appeasing all contradictions, seems to resolve the problem of theosophy; the magical activity of the pseudo-prophet Apollonius simulates a theurgy; finally, the solution of the economic problem, the advent of the universal empire and the pseudo-reunion of the churches constitutes a pseudo-theocracy, because God is replaced by Satan'.[69] William Desmond calls the reign of the Antichrist a 'parodia sacra', working with 'simulations of the highest values, which have been hollowed out'.[70] Yet even in this parody of all Solov'ëv's earlier hopes divine Wisdom continues to play a role: when the genuine Christian minority is at least unified in representatives of Catholicism, Orthodoxy and Protestantism, there is seen in the heavens the Woman clothed with the sun of chapter eight of the Book of Revelation.

But would such an end be an expression of 'Malkuth', the fruit of divine-human effort? In one sense, yes, for Solov'ëv, like the

Johannine Apocalypse, envisages two resurrections. The first—this at least is Solov'ëv's 'take' on St John the Divine—is entirely divine act, and only concerns Jews (pogroms against whom in tsarist Russia increasingly distressed him) and martyred Christians. Solov'ëv had 'always emphasized the historical interconnectedness of Christianity and Judaism, which is quite exceptional in a Russian-Orthodox context.'[71] In the course of the millennium that follows the first resurrection, divine-human efforts will bring about, at the millennium's close, the resurrection of all the dead, and this is a theurgic work *par excellence*.[72]

Solov'ëv fell seriously ill on 28 July (old calendar) 1900. As his suffering worsened he prayed intensely for the Jewish people (did his 'prophetic' gifts revive in pre-cognition of what the twentieth century would bring them?). After a three day wait his own sufferings came to their end. 'On his grave, next to an Orthodox ikon of the Resurrection with a Greek inscription, 'Christ has risen from the dead', was placed a Catholic ikon of the Blessed Virgin, with a Latin inscription, *In memoria aeterna erit justus*.'[73]

NOTES

1. Jonathan Sutton, 'Vladimir Solov'ëv as Reconciler and Polemicist', in van den Bercken, de Courten and van der Zweerde, *Vladimir Solov'ëv*, pp. 1–11, and here at p. 4.

2. Solowiew, *Vie de Vladimir Solowiew*, pp. 387–93. He was preceded in this exaggerated view by Michel d'Herbigny, *Un Newman russe. Vladimir Soloviev, 1853–1900* (Paris: Beauchesne, 1911).

3. James K. Zatko, *Descent into Darkness. The Destruction of the Roman Catholic Church in Russia, 1917–1923* (Notre Dame, IN: University of Notre Dame Press, 1965).

4. Nemeth, *The Later Solov'ëv*, pp. 110–16.

5. Strémooukhoff, *Vladimir Soloviev*, p. 273.

6. *Ibid.*, p. 267. For an account of Solov'ëv's aesthetic theories, see against the backcloth of earlier Russian 'philosophies of beauty', see Nemeth, *The Later Solov'ëv*, pp. 125–50.

7. *Ibid.*, p. 276.

8. Smith, *Vladimir Soloviev and the Spiritualization of Matter*, p. 2.

9. *The Meaning of Love* (London: Geoffrey Bles, 1945), p. 63.
10. *Ibid.*
11. Alice M. Hadfield, 'Introduction. The Writing of "Outlines of Romantic Theology"', in Charles Williams, *Outlines of Romantic Theology*, with which is reprinted *Religion and Love in Dante: The Theology of Romantic Love* (Berkeley, CA: Apocryphile Press, 2005), p. ix.
12. Charles Williams, *He Came Down from Heaven* (London: Heinemann, 1938), pp. 62–81.
13. Charles Williams, *Religion and Love in Dante: the Theology of Romantic Love* (Westminster: Dacre Press, 1941), reprinted in his *Outlines of Romantic Theology*, pp. 91–111.
14. Charles Williams, *The Figure of Beatrice. A Study in Dante* (London: Faber and Faber, 1943).
15. *Ibid.*, p. 15.
16. *Ibid.*, pp. 15–16.
17. *Ibid.*, p. 27.
18. *Ibid.*, p. 187.
19. *Ibid.*, p. 188.
20. Cited *ibid.*, p. 221.
21. *The Meaning of Love*, p. 22.
22. *Ibid.*
23. *Ibid.*, pp. 22–3.
24. *Ibid.*, p. 27.
25. *Ibid.*, pp. 33–4. Italics original.
26. *Ibid.*, p. 38.
27. *Ibid.*, p. 53.
28. *Ibid.*, p. 63.
29. *Ibid.*, pp. 56–64.
30. *Ibid.*, p. 57.
31. Thomas Nemeth, *Vladimir Solovy'ëv's Justification of the Moral Good* (Cham: Springer, 2015), p. li.
32. *Ibid.*, p. xxxiii.
33. *Ibid.*, p. xxviii.
34. Strémooukhoff, *Vladimir Soloviev*, p. 235.
35. Nemeth, *Vladimir Solovy'ëv's Justification of the Moral Good*, p. xl.
36. Strémooukhoff, *Vladimir Soloviev*, p. 257.

37. *Ibid.*
38. *Ibid.*, p. 262.
39. *Opravdanie dobra*, in Solov'ëv and Radlov, *Sobranie sochineniĭ*, VIII, pp. 3–516.
40. Strémooukhoff, *Vladimir Soloviev*, p. 237.
41. *Ibid.*
42. *Ibid.*, p. 241.
43. Nemeth, *Vladimir Solovy'ëv's Justification of the Moral Good*, p. 100. Italics original.
44. *Ibid.*
45. *Ibid.*, p. 101.
46. Strémooukhoof, *Vladimir Soloviev*, pp. 242–3.
47. Nemeth, *Vladimir Solov'ëv's Justification of the Moral Good*, p. 134.
48. *Ibid.*, p. 148.
49. *Ibid.*, p. 149.
50. *Ibid.*
51. *Ibid.*, p. 150.
52. *Ibid.*, p. 151.
53. *Ibid.*, p. 152.
54. *Ibid.*, pp. 165–6.
55. *Ibid.*, p. 166.
56. *Ibid.*
57. Strémooukhoof, *Vladimir Soloviev*, p. 244.
58. *Ibid.*, p. 215.
59. *Ibid.*
60. *Ibid.*, p. 366.
61. *Ibid.*, p. 387.
62. *Ibid.*, p. 407.
63. *Ibid.*, p. 413.
64. *Tri razgovora o voĭne, progresse i kontse vsemirnoĭ istorii, so vklyucheniem kratkoĭ povesti ob antikhriste*, in Solov'ëv and Radlov, *Sobranie sochineniĭ*, X, pp. 81–221. The French translation, *Trois entretiens sur la guerre, la morale et la religion* (Paris: Plon, 1916), includes a very full introduction.
65. *Ibid.*, p. LXXXIX.
66. von Balthasar, *The Glory of the Lord*, p. 290.

67. Strémooukhoof, *Vladimir Soloviev*, p. 283.
68. Smith, *Vladimir Soloviev and the Spiritualization of Matter*, p. 12.
69. Strémooukhoof, *Vladimir Soloviev*, p. 295.
70. Desmond, 'God beyond the Whole', p. 186. Desmond calls the Antichrist 'the worldly god of the whole', p. 189, and speculates that the *Legend* may have been Solov'ëv's act of penance for his one-time salutation of Auguste Comte's concept of the 'Grand Être', 'the last and ultimate community of Humanity … with its priesthood of scientists, its liturgical calendar of the great heroes of Humanity, and the supreme positivist Pontiff above it all', *ibid.*, p. 188.
71. van den Bercken, 'The Macrochristianity of Vladimir Solov'ëv', p. 67. This was especially evidenced in the eirenicism of his 1884 essay 'The Jews and the Christian Question': 'Evreistvo i khristianskii vopros', in Solov'ëv and Radlov, *Sobranie sochineniĭ*, IV, pp. 135–85.
72. Strémooukhoof, *Vladimir Soloviev*, p. 297.
73. Zouboff, 'Introduction', p. 28.

✣ 5 ✣

SOPHIOLOGY'S NEMESIS?

THE NEMESIS OF SOPHIOLOGY—though the question-mark in my chapter title indicates demolition was incomplete—bears a name. The counter-influence to the 'Sophiology Man', at least for English speakers and in the world of international academe, was Georges Florovsky. 'Florovsky advanced his neopatristic synthesis with a view to questioning and ultimately undermining the panentheistic ontology of Russian sophiology, epitomized in Solovyov's and Bulgakov's work.'[1] In his essay 'The Ways of Russian Theology' (not to be confused with the massive book of the same title), Florovsky made an appeal for Russian theologians to return to the Fathers, rather than pursue the will-o'-the-wisp of a new Christian intellectualism courtesy of the German Idealist philosophers (via Solov'ëv). As we have seen, Solov'ëv had made a study of the Fathers, but it is a rare thing for him actually to cite them.

The position was very different with Solov'ëv's premier theological disciple. Conscious, no doubt, of the considerable amount of patristic text woven into the fabric of Bulgakov's 'Great Trilogy', Florovsky used his essay to warn that this 'return' must be to the spirit, and not simply to the letter, of the Fathers' works. He may perhaps have had a traditionalist 'theology of repetition' chiefly in mind. But there was also in these words a covert recognition that the Diaspora theology influenced by the 'Religious Renaissance' of *fin-de-siècle* Russia where Solov'ëv's inspiration had been paramount, could scarcely be described as totally non-patristic. 'The debate between the generation of Bulgakov on the one hand and the generation of Florovsky on the other was not *whether* patristic theology was foundational—for both sides accepted that it was—but rather *how* to engage the patristic tradition this side of modernity.'²

Florovsky framed the general debate in terms of 'style and methods', with an emphasis on intuitive penetration of the deeper meaning and wider orientation of the texts and the testimonial value of the Fathers' confession of faith—their 'catholicity'.

> Our [i.e. Russia's] crisis of breaking away from Byzantium in the sixteenth century was an abandonment of Patristic tradition as well. There was no rupture within spiritual experience; on the contrary Russian piety, if we look back, appears even archaic. But theology had lost the Patristic style and methods. The works of the Fathers become archives, lifeless documents. It is not enough to be acquainted with the texts and to know how to draw from them quotes and arguments. One must possess the theology of the Fathers from within. Intuition is perhaps more important for this than erudition, for intuition alone revives their writings and makes them a *witness*. It is only from within that we can perceive and distinguish what (actually) is a catholic testimony from what would be merely theological opinion, hypothesis, interpretation, or theory... Reviving the Patristic style is the very promise of theological renaissance. This does not mean a restoration, a return to the past, nor a repetition. 'Returning to the Fathers' means, for all intents, to advance, not to go backwards. What we need is to be faithful to the spirit, not to the letter of the Fathers, to let ourselves be kindled at the flame of their fiery inspiration, not to gather specimens for a herbarium.³

This was the plea that gave the neo-patristic movement its war-cry: 'Forward to the Fathers!'

Florovsky made it plain he considered personal originality the very last thing theologians should prioritize.

> Those who, by reason of their humility in the presence of the Truth, have received the gift to express [the] *catholic*

consciousness of the Church, we call them Fathers and Doctors, since what they make us hear is not only their thought or their personal conviction, but moreover the very *witness* of the Church, for they speak from the depth of its catholic fullness. Their theology evolves on the plane of catholicity, of universal communion. And this is the first thing we must learn. Through asceticism and concentration, the theologian must learn to find his bearings *in* the Church: *Cor nostrum sit semper in Ecclesia* [Let our heart be always in the Church] ... We must be engrafted in the Church, in order to grow in it and live in that mysterious tradition, integral and trans-temporal, which embraces the sum of all revelations and visions. There, and there only, is the guaranty of creative work, and not in the seductive affirmation of a prophetic freedom.[4]

The negative use of the adjective 'prophetic' harks back, probably deliberately, to Solov'ëv's highly positive use, not only in his theocratic writings but also in connexion with the new intellectuality he called 'free theosophy'. 'The ideal of prophecy resonates across Solov'ëv's life and œuvre. From early on, he understood his vocation in prophetic terms, and consciously sought to position himself in a line of prophets from both the Russian literary and the Judeo-Christian traditions.'[5]

Yet at the same time—perhaps unconsciously—Florovsky echoed typically Solov'ëvan language in speaking of history as a 'theanthropic process'—a term emphasized by italicization in his printed text. 'The theologian must discover history as a *theanthropic process*, a pass-over from time to the eternity of grace, the becoming and the building of the Body of Christ.'[6] In his own way, Florovsky was no less interested in—and affected by—the philosophy of history than had been Solov'ëv.[7] Nor were his intellectual sources restricted to the Fathers (or the Bible). The surprising discovery of recent Florovsky research is the extent of his own indebtedness to the very 'Russian Religious Renaissance' to which his neo-patristic theology was formally counterposed. 'Both the questions that he asked of the patristic sources as well as the range of answers that he was prepared to entertain were guided by the main themes of the Renaissance.'[8]

Florovsky admitted Solov'ëv had been his own first master in religious philosophy. During his teenage years he considered Solov'ëv's notion of integral knowledge to be Russia's great gift to philosophy at large, and both the 'epistemology of integral knowledge and his metaphysics of all-unity ... in line with patristic theology'.[9] It was only through reading the contributions of Bulgakov, Berdyaev, Florensky, Evgeny Trubetskoy—in a letter of 1911, these are accounted the 'new Russian philosophers of the Solovyovan school'—that doubts began to arise in this precocious eighteen year old's mind.[10] What the principal historian of Florovsky's European career, Paul Gavrilyuk, terms the 'theosophical and mystical explorations' of these thinkers now set the alarm-bells ringing. Florovsky the young adult considered any 'form of religious experience not explicitly sanctioned by the Orthodox Church ... as a sort of spiritual minefield'—though, curiously, as Gavrilyuk points out, the mature Florovsky devoted remarkably little attention to describing that 'ecclesial experience' which was, for him, the chief source of Christian doctrine.[11]

Perhaps he took its meaning for granted. In its more immediate sense, it surely meant inhabiting Orthodoxy's worshipping life. And Florovsky clearly understood this already to entail spiritual sobriety and the avoidance of theological idiosyncracies. More widely, as Gavrilyuk himself concedes, 'The "living experience of the Church", as Florovsky uses the expression, is not a separate source of the knowledge of God, but rather a set of historical practices that reliably mediate the content of divine revelation, enshrined in scripture and tradition'.[12]

For Florovsky the Russian theology of the early twentieth century was still at a learning stage. In its pupilage it had not yet earned the right to put forward masters of its own. The emergence of, say, a Bulgakov was premature. As he wrote in 'The Ways of Russian Theology':

> It would not be correct to say that Russian theology, in its creative development, has perceived and assimilated completely or deeply enough the Fathers and Byzantium. This it must still do. It must pass through the austere schooling of Christian Hellenism. Hellenism, so to speak, assumed a perpetual character in the Church; it has incorporated itself in the very fabric of the Church as the *eternal category* of Christian existence.[13]

To preclude possible misunderstandings (unsuccessfully, for these have been noted among Florovsky's followers in Greece and the Greek Diaspora[14]) he added,

> Of course what is meant here is not that ethnical Hellenism of modern Hellas or of the Levant, nor Greek phyletism, which is obsolete and without justification. We are dealing with Christian antiquity, with the Hellenism of dogma, of the liturgy, of the icon ... All the errors and temptations of a Hellenization forwarded indiscreetly—they happened repeatedly in the course of history—cannot possibly weaken the significance of this fundamental fact: the 'good news' and Christian theology, once and for all, were expressed from the start in Hellenistic categories. Patristic [*sic*] and catholicity, historicity and Hellenism are the joint aspects of a unique and indivisible datum.[15]

Florovsky considered in advance a possible objection. In this Hellenocentric vision what has happened to Israel's sacred Scriptures, the Christian 'Old Testament', and, for that matter, to the Hebraic heritage of the New? We might recall here the high place given to the Judaic patrimony by Solov'ëv.[16] Florovsky countered by saying, 'The truth of "Hebraism" is included in the Hellenic synthesis. Hellenism was integrated into the Church precisely through the Biblical engrafting. It is impossible, even from a historical point of view, to justify the opposition between "Semitism" and "Hellenism".'[17] For Florovsky the Old Testament was not merely included within the Greek patristic synthesis. It was absorbed without remainder.

'The Old Testament no longer belongs to the Jews. It belongs to the Church alone.'[18] It is unlikely that the author of 'The Jews and the Christian Question' would have endorsed this comment. Solov'ëv wrote there, 'we are separated from Jews because we are not yet fully Christians, and they from us because they are not yet fully Jews. For the fullness of Christianity embraces Judaism as well, and the fullness of Judaism is Christianity.'[19]

For Florovsky, then, there was no good biblical reason to relativize 'Christian Hellenism'—nor, as he now went on to explain, was there any ecclesial justification for its replacement or, less radically, supplementation by German Idealism.

> When German idealism conquered the hearts, some scholars devised to transpose all the dogmatics and even the dogmas from the allegedly obsolete language of Hellenism into the idioms, more intelligible and actual of the new idealism, in the manner of Hegel, Schelling, Baader, and their like (Khomiakov himself had thought to do that) ... [Yet] 'modern philosophy and theology' must first be submitted to a test and a justification, the criterion of which is rooted in the depths of ecclesiastical experience. And there is no common measure between the latter and the methods of Hegel or Kant.[20]

Florovsky's closing statement is indubitably true, though it raises the question of how *any* philosophy of an autonomous—that is, revelation-independent—kind can enter in an auxiliary capacity into revelation's service.

In Florovsky's opinion, the sophiologists' appeal for a re-statement of the truths of the Creed by making use of the categories of Idealism was not only no real improvement on classical philosophy. Rather was it a retrogressive move. Had the proposal been adopted throughout Orthodox theological culture all that the Fathers had ever done to baptize the philosophy of the ancient world would have gone. This claim presumes that German Lutheran sources (say, Schelling) or German Catholic sources (say, Baader) would relate to 'sacred Hellenism' by way of 'replacement' rather than 'supplement'—though the latter term reflects more accurately the views of Solov'ëv, and for that matter Kireevsky, from whose cup Solov'ëv had drunk deep. In Florovsky's view, the effect of such ill-advised interference with the body of Christian thought would be to reinstate certain proto-Idealist elements found in the ancient philosophical heritage itself. 'German idealism itself was nothing else but a backsliding into pre-Christian idealism.'[21] Paul Gavrilyuk well sums up the abiding advantages of a Christianized Hellenic philosophy in Florovsky's eyes. 'The ahistorical cosmism of the Greeks gave way to the mighty acts of God in history; the conception of [a] divinized eternal cosmos was replaced with the intuition of the creature's time-bound contingency and dependence upon God; the metaphysical primacy of the universal over [the] individual was challenged by Christianity's emphasis upon the uniqueness of persons; the deterministic accounts of divine and human agency were rejected in favour of safeguarding divine freedom and human cooperation with divine grace.'[22] Here Florovsky's view that Christian Hellenism had already proved its credentials as the providentially provided philosophical prop for Orthodox theology mirrored the contemporary claims of Western neo-mediaeval apologists for the 'perennial philosophy' of the Scholastics as the necessary and sufficient philosophical support for Latin Catholicism. A text like Étienne Gilson's *The Elements of Christian Philosophy* could well form the basis for a pertinent comparison.[23]

One thing, however, Florovsky *did* share with Solov'ëv at the time of writing 'The Ways of Russian Theology'. This was the desire for a new engagement of Orthodoxy with the West. 'We must not merely refute and reject Western pronouncements and errors, but rather overcome them through a new creative activity.'[24] For Florovsky, Solov'ëv's mind was not so much over-immersed in Western thought as insufficiently abreast of it to set out a suitable programme in this respect. 'Soloviev was less familiar with the West [than were Gogol or Dostoevsky], less aware of its inconsistencies and contradictions, obsessed as he was with "Christian politics". In fact, he knew very little of the West, besides ultramontanism and German idealism (one should add perhaps [the Utopian Socialist] Fourier, [the eccentric Lutheran visionary] Swedenborg, the spiritualists and, among the ancient masters, Dante).'[25] In Florovsky's view, Solov'ëv's theocratic concerns had over-politicized his approach to what by Florovsky's own day was termed the 'ecumenical question'. 'Soloviev dealt with the nation's calling, the theocratic mission of the Russian Empire, rather than with the mission of Orthodoxy.'[26] This final observation was undoubtedly correct.

Florovsky wanted Orthodox theology to engage more fully with the texts and monuments of the Western Christian tradition—partly, yes, so as to understand what had gone wrong in the development of Latin Christendom, but also to appreciate, with some justice, what had gone right.

> *New theology*, in order to refute errors, must be informed by a *historiosophic exegesis* of the religious tragedy of the West. However, such an exegesis must be tested; we must make it our own, and show that it can undergo *catharsis* in the fullness of ecclesial experience and of Patristic tradition. In the new Orthodox synthesis, the centuries old experience of the West must be taken into consideration and studied with more attention and sympathy than our theologians ever did thus far. This does not mean that we should borrow nor adopt Roman doctrines, and indulge in romanizing mimesis [as Solov'ëv had done by accepting the 'Petrine claims', and Bulgakov, in the process of leaving Russia during the Civil War, had for a while considered doing likewise[27]]. What I try to say is that Orthodox thought shall, at any rate, find a better source of creative inspiration in the great systems of higher scholasticism, in the experience of the western mystics and in the theology of modern Catholicism, than in German idealism, in the Protestant critique of past centuries or of the present, or even in contemporary 'dialectical theology'.[28]

Solov'ëv had been looking to the wrong interlocutors—whether marginal or dubiously orthodox texts from the Christian West, or Ultramontane clergy like the Parisian Jesuits, or the occasional Pan-Slavist Latin bishop, such as Strossmayer. Florovsky's list of suitable interlocutors (described in categories rather than *nominatim*) bore no resemblance to Solov'ëv's. It was a surprising one, for Florovsky did not say, as many twentieth- and twenty-first-century Orthodox might, that the 'interlocutors' should be for preference (if not exclusively) the Latin Fathers and ecclesiastical writers of the pre-Schism epoch. Rather, Florovsky sought an Orthodox use of the doctors and divines of the Latin West far beyond the dating of the Schism—he was appealing for the Orthodox to read and make use of Thomas and Bonaventure, Bernard of Clairvaux and Catherine of Siena, and such moderns as Emile Mersch, Henri de Lubac, Romano Guardini (these are my guesses: Florovsky did not himself specify these exemplary names).

In this recommendation, Florovsky was assuming in the Roman Catholic Church the continuance of a sustained and hegemonic attention to its own heritage—an attention that, in the 1950s and '60s, began to lose focus through an increasingly unilateral concern with *aggiornamento*, or 'updating'—a concept whose evangelical downside (is it a capitulation to the times?) was already noted by Karl Barth in his comments on the Second Vatican Council before the 1960s had ended.[29] Half a century later, it was more difficult to recognize in Florovsky's generous description of tradition-mindedness in the Catholic West the realities of the Latin church on the ground.

> The fact that the conscience of the West is constantly attentive to the ecclesial reality of history, that it assumes a responsible and heedful attitude toward it, that it never desists from reflecting meditating on the Christian sources, this fact already is important. Western thought continues to live in that past, thereby compensating, so to speak, the weakness of its mystical memory with the liveliness of its recollections. To the western world, the Orthodox theologian himself must bring its witness, the witness of the intimate memory of the Church, in order to have it coincide with the results of historical research. It is only that intimate memory of the Church which vitalizes fully the silent witness of the texts.[30]

What is Florovsky saying here? Surely that contemporary Orthodox ecclesial consciousness, once intuitively re-attuned (where necessary) to the patristic ethos, must then transmute materials made available from Christian history so as to make them speak again—or even sing! Where these materials derive from the tradition of the Latin church, this will be the 'harmonization' Solov'ëv had desired, even if, in and of itself, it does not amount to ecclesial reunion, Solov'ëv's pole star.

In Part One of the book-length *The Ways of Russian Theology*, a comprehensive history of Russian theology and not simply an analysis of the latter's deficiencies in its author's eyes, Florovsky used the Preface to reaffirm his basic credo. (The book must of course be distinguished from the essay of the same name already discussed.)

> All the genuine achievements of Russian theology were always linked with a creative return to patristic sources. That this narrow path of patristic theology is the sole way is revealed with particular clarity in historical perspective. Yet the return to the fathers must not be solely intellectual or historical, it must be a return in spirit and prayer, a living and creative self-restoration to the fullness of the Church in the entirety of sacred tradition ... [A] genuine awakening can only begin when not only the answers but the questions are heard in the past and in the future. The inexhaustible power of patristic tradition in theology is defined still more by the fact that theology was a matter of life for the holy fathers, a spiritual quest (*podvig*), a confession of faith, a creative resolution of living tasks. The ancient books were always inspired with this creative spirit.[31]

Here Florovsky claimed for his own neo-patristic project no less theological creativity than Bulgakov had asserted (and exemplified) for sophiology. 'Orthodoxy is once again revealed in patristic exegesis as a conquering power, as the power giving rebirth and affirmation to life, not only as a way station for tired and disillusioned souls; not only as the end but as the beginning, the beginning of a quest and creativity, a "new creature".'[32] Gavrilyuk has noted, however, a curious phenomenon. 'The assumptions that Florovsky brought to bear upon his historical analysis of the development of Russian

Orthodox theology—that Russia's encounter with Byzantium led to authentic development of native culture and that the encounter with the West brought about a pseudomorphosis—were first formulated in his conversations with his Eurasian colleagues and with [Nikolaï] Trubetskoy in particular.'[33] The 'Eurasians', writing in the early 1920s, had argued for the integration of Russian culture with that of Central Asia.[34] By the end of the decade, however, Florovsky had broken with the group, sharing its anti-Latinism (but not its Asiatic proclivities) and deploring its downplaying of human freedom as a shaper of history, rather than such factors as climate and landscape. Still, the main lines of his Orientalizing—better, Byzantinizing—critique of the Russian religious thought inherited from the tsardom were already apparent.

In Part One of *The Ways of Russian Theology* Florovsky furnished some important background to the Schellingianism that played so notable a part in Solov'ëv's lifelong conceptual experimentalism. The appeal to conspiratorial 'Freemasonic influence' as an explanation for the inner hollowing out of Church traditions has become tiresomely common among Traditionalist critics of post-Conciliar Western Catholicism. Yet Florovsky was on secure historical ground in invoking the influence of the Lodge in late-eighteenth- and early-nineteenth-century Russia.

> Freemasonry did not limit itself to a culture of the heart. Freemasonry had its own metaphysics and dogmatics. Its metaphysics made freemasonry an anticipation and premonition of Romanticism and Romantic *Naturphilosophie*. The experience of the Moscow Rosicrucians (and later of Freemasonry during Alexander I's reign) prepared the soil for the development of Russian Schellingianism ... which germinated from these same magical roots. Two motifs are important in this magical mysticism, this 'divine alchemy'. The first is the vital feeling for world harmony or universal unity, the wisdom of the world and the mystical apprehension of nature.... The second motif is a vivid anthropocentric self-awareness: man as the 'extract of all beings.'[35]

It is not difficult to see in these words two principal themes of Solov'ëv's writing: *vseedinstvo* and Sophia herself on the one hand, and the 'primordial humanity' of the all-creating Logos on the other. There is nothing here, however, about the role of a philosophy of history—key to Solov'ëv's thought and, to Copleston's mind, the principal attraction of Orthodox Russians to the German thinker. Schelling is presented as one who ruminated not so much on history as on nature—yet nature and history can hardly be separated in Schelling's own thought.

Be that as it may: for Florovsky, nineteenth-century Russian philosophy became so ambitiously religious as to constitute a simulacrum of religion in its own right. Thus in Part Two of *The Ways of Russian Theology*, after giving the Church schools their due in instilling in their students the elements of a philosophical culture,[36] he went on to find in the University of Moscow of the period the beginnings of an altogether inflated view of the services philosophy could render. The 'Society of Wisdom-Lovers [*Obshchestvo lyubomudriya*] stood first in the succession of circles ... The love of wisdom itself became their new religion; philosophy took on a religious pathos and became a religious substitute.'[37] And he added what was for him a damning finale, 'The stamp of romanticism is quite evident in all this.'[38] The English literary critic T. E. Hulme, once defined Romanticism as 'spilt religion.'[39] Florovsky would have concurred.

Unlike Solov'ëv's chief disciples he had little time for attempts after the 'revolution' of 1905 to reform the life of the Russian church and to reinvigorate the appeal to the intelligentsia made at the turn of the century. The approach of the reformers was deeply shallow. 'Few acknowledged the need for a spiritual awakening; few understood that the restoration of inner peace and order could not be achieved by church politics, but only through spiritual and ascetic exploit (*podvig*). The only way out was precisely in ascetic recollection or renaissance.'[40] He pondered Nicolas Berdyaev's opinion that the 'Russian Religious Renaissance'—the term popularized by another Nicolas, Nicolas Zernov—was too narrowly based in the cultural elite, with insufficient time to expand its influence before, in 1917, a more far-reaching revolution supervened.[41] In Florovsky's judgment, far more damaging had been the narrowness of the historical base.

> The Russian religious 'renaissance', strictly speaking, was only a return to the experience of German idealism and German mysticism. For some it meant a return to Schelling or Hegel, for others to Jakob Boehme, and for still others to Goethe. The increasingly powerful influence of Soloviev only served to reinforce the enchantment with German philosophy, while the actual expanses of church history remained virtually unknown. The history of the ancient Church was customarily perceived through the images and interpretations of German historians. Even classical philosophy was received through German mediation. Overly pronounced echoes of estheticism and symbolism still remained lodged in the very sense of history.[42]

Florovsky's encylopaedic knowledge of Russian scholarship gives this negative assessment some prima facie credibility. And his knowledge of the wider European scene in the nineteenth century enabled him to venture a further judgment affecting, this time, not only the originality of the 'Russian Religious Renaissance' but also its utility—at any rate from a Church standpoint. 'It is customary to speak of contemporary Russian philosophy as if it were a uniquely creative product of the Russian spirit. This is completely false, for, on the contrary, the substitution of "religious philosophy" for theology characterized all western romanticism, especially the German variety. This was also the case with the Catholic speculative philosophy of the romantic period. In all this was one of the most western episodes in Russia's development.'[43] As to Berdyaev personally—the most prominent of the surviving religious philosophers of the epoch— he was, for Florovsky, 'totally in the grip of German mystical visions, which cut him off from the life of the Great Church.'[44] The 'Vladimir Solov'ëv Religious-Philosophical Society' founded in Moscow in 1907 might have included Bulgakov and Florensky, but they were the only two who went on to become theologians (and Orthodox priests to boot).

In that setting, Evgeniĭ Trubetskoy had been, for Florovsky, the 'most faithful upholder' of Solov'ëv's tradition, but, more importantly—granted Trubetskoy's early death and the relatively minor character of his contribution—Solov'ëv 'had a decisive influence on the spiritual development of Bulgakov', and Bulgakov was to become the theological giant of the post-Revolutionary diaspora.[45] Bulgakov, remarks Florovsky, 'accepted Soloviev's doctrine of Sophia, which became the basis of his entire system. The same is true of Florenskiĭ'.[46] The influence of Solov'ëv on Bulgakov is undeniable. Had he not declared Solov'ëv's philosophy to be 'the last word of world philosophical thought, its highest synthesis'?[47] But otherwise these statements were simplifications unworthy of a fine historian of thought.

In the specifically theological works he produced (the Little Trilogy, the Great Trilogy—the pre-Revolutionary economic and philosophical writings, including *Unfading Light*, are another matter[48]), Bulgakov's version of Sophiology differs from Solov'ëv's in at least three respects. He seeks to confine his source material to what is usual in Orthodox theology. He operates with a clear distinction between Wisdom as the divine *ousia* and Wisdom as the reflection of the divine mind in creation. He 'de-feminizes' Wisdom, thus sundering it from the 'Eternal Feminine' imagery of the wider European literary tradition. As to Florensky, a glance at his principal work, *The Pillar and the Ground of Truth*, shows that sophiological thinking only appears in the last of the 'Letters' of which the book is composed, a sign of what appears to be sophiology's comparatively reduced role in his overall achievement—though much of Florensky's output has only trickled out, from the family archives, since the end of the Communist era and awaits a comprehensive analysis. At any rate, the leading Italian scholar in Florensky studies, Natalino Valentini, can write a study of 'Faces of the Russian Soul' disproportionately indebted to Florensky's writing that nevertheless manages to avoid sophiology entirely.[49]

Sophiology's Nemesis?

The figure of Solov'ëv is absolutely crucial to Florovsky's account of the wrong turning of recent (i.e. twentieth-century) Russian theology. He wrote:

> The influence of philosophy is especially clear in the systematic construction of Russian 'secular theologians'— the Slavophiles and Khomiakov, but especially Vladimir Solov'ev and his followers. The close connection between the religio-philosophical *Weltanschauung* and quest of Vladimir Solov'ev with German idealist philosophy, especially with Schelling, partly with Baader, Schopenhauer, and Ed[uard] von Hartmann is completely obvious. Solov'ev's system, however, was an attempt to re-shape afresh the dogmas of Christian belief and tradition in the categories of modern philosophy, a task which had already concerned Khomiakov. From Solov'ev this tradition, taken up by his spiritual followers and successors, passed into the contemporary religio-philosophical tradition. To such an understanding of theological tasks one should oppose another: the task of theology lies not so much in translating the Tradition of faith into contemporary language, into the terms of the most recent philosophy, but lies rather in discovering in the ancient patristic tradition the perennial principles of Christian philosophy; this task lies not in controlling dogma by means of contemporary philosophy but rather in re-shaping philosophy on the experience of faith itself so that the experience of faith would become the source and measure of philosophical views. The weakest side of Solov'ev and his school was precisely this misuse of the speculative process which can enchain, and often even deform, Tradition and the experience of faith. The influence of German philosophy, in any case, organically penetrated Russian theological consciousness.[50]

This, if by now repetitive, was not an unbalanced summary, and indeed Florovsky could be at points a not only fair but positive, if not exactly enthusiastic, expositor of Solov'ëv's writings. In Part

Two of *The Ways of Russian Theology*, he wrote sympathetically of at least two aspects of Solov'ëv's thought. These were, first, Solov'ëv's desire for a Christianity that would transform all realms of human life—which can hardly exclude the realm of thought, and secondly, his attitude to what in the West came to be called, after Newman, the 'development of doctrine'.

I look now at the *first* of these—what we might term the 'omni-transformative' nature of the Christian vocation. Florovsky noted how 'in the social radicalism of his time Solov'ev perceived a quest for a transfigured world'.[51] A confused or blind quest for truth must be brought to Christ. The Church 'must "raise ['this mysterious current of rediscovered truth'] to the highest degree of rational consciousness", and place it firmly in a higher and transfigured synthesis'.[52] Florovsky added, rightly enough: 'Solov'ëv firmly believed that the Church could attain its fullness and fulfillment only in historical action. And, conversely, historical creativity or construction first receives its real justification and support only in the Church, i.e. in the truth of Godmanhood'.[53] The regeneration of humanity and the wider world in the spirit of Christ by the transformation of earth into the Kingdom of God, which is not of this world, was Solov'ëv's 'firm and unalterable belief; the core of his entire system'.[54]

Philosophy just had to come into this 'omni-transformative' picture, since 'philosophy must prepare or substantiate this great synthesis, this "total-unity" (*vse-edinstvo*), this great and new restoration'.[55] In Solov'ëv's judgment, what appeared to be the irrationality of Christianity was 'the chief cause of unbelief and apostasy' in the modern age. 'For this reason he attached the highest importance to creating an adequate form for disclosing Christian truth, to the "justification of the faith of the fathers", through philosophy. In its entirety, his philosophy claimed to be precisely such a confession of the Christian faith in the element of truth'.[56] Traditional theology, on Solov'ëv's analysis, is partly responsible for the apostasy in that it 'does not include empirical knowledge of nature or give a creative horizon to reason'.[57] Florovsky recalled the goal of Solov'ëv's theosophic synthesis: to unite theology, philosophy and science in a way that would organize in satisfying fashion the entire realm of knowledge. Florovsky could write admiringly of features of this project—and even of its historic upshot within the intellectual life of Orthodoxy. It was 'at one and the same time a return to metaphysics and a return to dogma. It was also a reaction to every form of psychologism, pietism, and moralism.'[58]

What then, *au fond*, is the problem with the Solov'ëvan enterprise so described? Florovsky replies, 'Soloviev's basic and fatal contradiction lies in the fact that he attempted to construct an ecclesiastical synthesis from non-ecclesiastical experience. This applies above all to his fundamental conception—his doctrine of Sophia. Subsequently he always remained in the stifling and constricted circle of theosophy and Gnosticism. After the collapse of his unionist-utopian hopes and calculations in the 1890s, he once again suffered a very painful relapse of this dreamy Gnosticism.'[59] For Florovsky, Solov'ëv was

> always more firmly and closely linked to neo-Platonism and modern German mysticism than to the experience of the Great Church and Catholic mysticism. Particularly characteristic is his complete lack of sensitivity to the liturgy. He saw the Church more in its scholastic and canonical elements, more on the level of 'Christian politics', and least of all on its mystical level, in its sacramental and spiritual depths. He had visions unattainable by the intellect (note his 'Three Encounters' and all of his mystical poetry in general), and yet it was precisely in these enigmatic 'encounters' and visions of 'Eternal Femininity' that he was furthest from the Church [which is true if Balthasar's Marian explanation of the encounters is excluded]. The *sobornost'* of the Church itself remained a closed mystery to him. He was too closely tied to Protestantism, through philosophy and through idealism and mysticism.[60]

Yet Florovsky cannot deny that Solov'ëv—not least by frequenting lectures at the Moscow Theological Academy, where he was a contemporary of Florovsky's father, Vasiliĭ Antonovich Florovsky—

had acquired to some degree a Church culture, and even a specifically patristic one. 'Of course he studied and gained a sufficient knowledge of the history of the ancient Church and the Holy Fathers.'[61] If so, the further comment that 'it seems he read Mansi more than Migne'—in other words, texts of Conciliar definitions, decrees, discussions (edited by Giovanni Domenico Mansi) rather than the life-giving words of the Fathers themselves (as re-published by Jacques-Paul Migne)—seems either self-contradictory or snide. But that engaged reading, though Florovsky found it meritorious, could not redeem the sin of Solov'ëv's attraction to Gnosticism, notably of the Valentinian sort, and (adds Florovsky) of Philo—whose 'influence is always discernible in Solov'ëv's interpretations of the Old Testament and in *The History and Future of Theocracy*.'[62] Florovsky was right that, with regard to the Old Testament, Solov'ëv was a ferocious allegorizer. He admits, though, Solov'ëv was not worse than Origen. In fact he was rather better since 'after being powerfully attracted by it he rejected Origenist "universalism"'.[63] Florovsky concludes that 'in a certain sense he remained in the pre-Nicaean era, with its propadeutic problematic', even though Solov'ëv makes perfectly plain, not least in the *Lectures on Godmanhood* and in *The Spiritual Foundations of Life*, his adhesion to not only Nicaea but also the succeeding ecumenical Councils, notably Chalcedon and Constantinople II and III in their Christological determinations.[64]

'Strangely enough', added Florovsky, 'Soloviev spoke much more about Godmanhood than about the God-man.'[65] That is true insofar as Solov'ëv's theosophic, theocratic and theourgic aims concern the extension of 'Godmanhood' from the God-man to the rest of the human creation (without of course the union of natures, which is unique to the person of the incarnate Word). Whether it is correct to say that 'in his system the image of the Saviour remained only a pale shadow', and to call the Christological chapters in the *Lectures on Godmanhood* 'completely undeveloped' is more dubious. The reader may well be content to accept at face value Solov'ëv's assignation to the Seven Councils of the task of painting a fuller Christological picture. Moreover, the case can be made that Solov'ëv's sophiology is actually Christologically focussed, and his Christology a unique version of Chalcedonianism whose characteristic concern, drawing on concepts from both Idealism and ancient Gnosis, is not to leave the Uncreated and the created elements in Christ simply juxtaposed.[66] Solov'ëv's 'Godmanhood' cannot be thought of without the God-man, for 'it is the union, achieved in Christ, of things divine and things human, of spirit and matter, of eternity and time. It is the culmination of evolution, the beginning of the deification of mankind and the world.'[67] Solov'ëv may only occasionally employ the terms 'redemption' (*iskuplenie*) and 'salvation (*spasenie*), but he makes copious use of the language of 'deification' (*obozhestvlenie*), 'transformation' (*preobrazovanie*) and 'rebirth' (*pererozhdenie*) of humanity and its world.[68] Admittedly, there is little here about the individual person's relation with the Saviour. In the words of the Dutch Russianist Wil van den Bercken, 'the macro-aspects prevail.'[69]

Is Florovsky correct to ascribe to Solov'ëv the view that 'Godmanhood has been realized from the beginning in the "eternal world", and the incarnation is only a certain manifestation of this eternal unity in the material and temporal world'?[70] In Florovsky's interpretation, the Incarnation is for Solov'ëv 'only a descent of the eternal Christ into the flow of phenomena'.[71] This exegesis of Lecture XI of Solov'ëv's text would be fair enough if the adverb 'only', used twice in the passage cited, were removed. (Indeed, the second of the two sentences quoted would be Solov'ëv verbatim were the offending adverb taken away.[72]) Yes, the Logos, for Solov'ëv, contains 'primordial humanity' within its own uncreated life. But for this divine 'Beginning' to be united with the quite non-divine 'beginning' of natural man there must take place a union between two natures (and two wills) in a single Personality which will entail, for that Personality, a twofold renunciation—kenotic self-restraint for the divine nature and the free submission to the divine of its human counterpart. This for Solov'ëv (using, as it happens, one of Florovsky's own most favoured words), is *podvig*—'an exploit, and a double exploit', a wonder of self-abnegation on both the divine and the human sides,[73] which is not deprived of its marvellous character by the fact that, in Solov'ëv's view, divine Providence had been preparing for this moment through cosmic aeons and historic generations.[74]

The 'descent... into the flow of phenomena' is no mere Docetic appearance. Its price for the Logos is measured by the struggle of the Temptations and the Passion of Christ. It is difficult to find in Lecture XI of the *Lectures on Godmanhood* verification of Florovsky's claim that 'Soloviev ... had moved far away from church dogma. All of his constructions have a powerful aftertaste of symbolical illusionism'.[75]

Where Florovsky definitely oversteps the mark is in his discussion of the Holy Trinity in the *Lectures on Godmanhood*. Solov'ëv does not in fact say that the difference between, on the one hand, the Church Fathers with their Trinitarianism and, on the other, pre-Christian adherents to a triadic account of ultimate reality is a mere matter of detail. Rather he holds that Christians—beginning with the apostles—*actually experienced*, in the mysteric events of the New Testament, that selfsame Word and Spirit whom in diverse ways Philo and the Neo-Platonists had hypothesized as theological or philosophical postulates.

So much for the sixth chapter of *The Ways of Russian Theology*, 'Philosophical Awakening'. In the following chapter, 'The Historical School', Florovsky broaches the question of the evolution of dogma. Like most, if not all, Orthodox theologians, Florovsky was not enamoured of the notion of doctrinal development.[76] But he was perfectly at ease with the idea of 'living tradition'. It was in the 1870s, so Florovsky points out, in dialogue with Old Catholics, that Russian theologians found themselves obliged to consider the notion that doctrinal innovations may become 'ecumenical'—but only as a typical aberration of the Roman see, signed and sealed in the Vatican Decrees of 1869–70. Both Orthodox and Old Catholics opposed thereto the principle of Tradition: appeal to the faith of the undivided Church as expressed at the patristic Councils. 'The question of "dogmatic development" was again raised with a new urgency in the 1880s by Vladimir Soloviev—once more in this same "Roman" context, as a means of justifying the dogmatic development of the teachings of the Roman Church.'[77] Florovsky felt the polemical context of Solov'ëv's comments had discouraged further enquiry. 'Soloviev's truth, however, lay in his living sense of the sacred reality of history in the Church.'[78] He saw that when the Body of Christ was first constituted, everything was given it, yet not everything was manifested. In this sense, the seed must become the full plant. Florovsky comments that 'this organic wholeness or catholicity is peculiarly characteristic of ecclesiastical development.'[79] And he recalls how 'Soloviev had already spoken of this in *The Spiritual Foundations of Life*, without any reference to the problem of uniting the churches. In this book he does not refer specifically to "dogmatic development", but only establishes a general principle,'[80] namely that nothing new can contradict the old since the same Holy Spirit acts uninterruptedly in the Church provided that people do not act in their own name but in that of the whole Church, visible and invisible, of past, present and future. In *The History and Future of Theocracy*, Solov'ëv had returned to the same subject but never going beyond the celebrated *Commonitorium* of Vincent of Lérins, which had suggested both the organic metaphor (seed and plant) and how homogeneity in such development is a sine qua non. The 'pledge of faith' remains inviolate and unaltered, the Church in no way adds to the 'inner truth' of the 'dogmatic propositions', yet their meaning is rendered clearer for her members.[81] On this question of the Church-in-history, 'Soloviev left behind an incontestable methodological service. Only by the historical or "genetic" method can a system of ecclesiology be constructed ... Above all, [the dogmatician] must spiritually perceive the question that each dogma answers.'[82]

But, these positive or at least not wholly negative notes sounded, Florovsky returns to Solov'ëv again—once more in the manner of his own, hyper-critical, earlier writing. Solov'ëv was disappointed by the failure of his theocratic scheme. But he did not for all that disclaim his notions of church reunion. Instead he took to apocalyptic. Believers will become a minority but they must combine in the interests of truth. Yet Florovsky believed the Soloviev of the early 1890s to have 'somehow internally left the [Orthodox] Church',[83] doing so in a frenzy of 'passionate theosophical love' as reflected in his *The Meaning of Love* (1892–4), 'a dreadful occult plan for the union of humanity with God through heterosexual love'.[84] There was an ominous return of concern with the *das Ewig-Weibliche*. In an essay of 1896 Solov'ëv spoke of the 'feminine Shadow of the Divinity', the 'eternally young Tsar [surely 'Tsarina'?]-Virgin'. In *The Meaning of Love* he registered a need for redirection of the eros that leads to it to better ends than animal reproduction. A 'sombre romantic-erotic thread' was woven into even his *The Justification of the Good*. An increase in magical motifs can be noted, yet in 1898 he had returned to theological topics, with some fixation on the Antichrist and the conviction that the reunion of Christians will come only with the End of all things. Florovsky asked whether Solov'ëv had become concerned with Christian values in place of Christ. One is surprised that a reader of *The Legend of the Antichrist* felt the need to put that question. The 'sacred parody' of the reign of Antichrist largely *consists* for Solov'ëv in replacing Christ by values.

Solov'ëv's contemporaries, so Florovsky points out, saw him as a philosopher, the younger generation as a mystic. The poet Aleksandr Blok continued his teaching on Sophia, replacing Solov'ëv's rationalism (*sic*) with 'alogical lyricism',[85] while Solov'ëv himself was deeply embarrassed by his unwanted visitor, Anna Shmidt—a figure connected with Blok—who considered herself the incarnation of Sophia as Solov'ëv of the Logos. For Florovsky, 'the development of Solov'evan themes by Blok and others serves as an immanent critique (and exposure) of his experiment, and calls into question all "religion of romanticism", religious estheticism, or esthetic religion ... Some enter the Church not to pray but to dream. And the religious life of those among the Russian intelligentsia who returned to the Church was stricken and poisoned by this temptation.'[86]

Yet paradoxically Florovsky, who saw the St Petersburg 'Religious-Philosophical Meetings of 1901–3' as of historic importance, speaking of their 'happy and totally unexpected success', considered that their theme was Solov'ëv's': 'only expressed more emphatically: while proclaiming heaven, the Church does not neglect the earth'.[87]

Writing elsewhere on 'Reason and Faith in the Philosophy of Solov'ev',[88] Florovsky considered that 'for Soloviev, "Religion", "Metaphysics", and "Science", are in no sense just "stages", but rather permanent categories of human existence, and none could be eliminated, if man was expected to continue in his essential humanity.'[89] The vocabulary suggests Florovsky had Auguste Comte, the founder of Positivism, in mind. Solov'ëv would have concurred in the need to combat the Comtian scheme of things—which he did robustly enough in his early writing even if, unfelicitously, he later borrowed Comte's phrase 'Great Humanity' as a quasi-synonym for the eternal humanity of God. 'Of course, Soloviev was fully aware of that sharp conflict between faith and reason which has been especially accentuated in modern times. But in his interpretation, this very conflict was precisely a necessary step in the development towards a free integration.'[90]

> His conviction that 'faith' and 'reason' should ultimately agree on all points was rooted in his metaphysical conception. In a sense, they are bound to diverge, when practiced as 'detached principles'. But, on the other hand, they must 'coincide', when brought together, in a wider and 'synthetic' perspective, in the context of the 'integral knowledge' ... And, secondly, for Soloviev, 'reason', strictly speaking, has no content, by and in itself. 'Reason' is a *formal principle*; it has no independent access to reality. It is, as it were, *essentially abstract*, i.e. precisely *'detached'* from reality', i.e. from the being. It is imprisoned in itself. It cannot ascertain reality, and in this sense it is blind. It cannot ascertain existence, unless it is made available to it by other means. On the contrary, 'faith' is precisely an insight into existence. It touches reality, even if it cannot, by itself, give an account of what is possesses. At this point, Soloviev walks in the steps of the later Schelling, with his strict distinction between a 'negative' philosophy, purely rational, and a 'positive', of which the first is inescapably 'formal', and the latter supplies an existential content out of the religious experience. One may again compare Soloviev's

contention with what Bergson had to say on the relationship between *instinct* and *intellect*. Bergson opposes 'the *material* knowledge of instinct' to 'the *formal* knowledge of intelligence', and concludes: *'there are things which intelligence alone is able to seek, but which, by itself, it will never find; these things instinct alone could find, but it will never seek them.'* It is along a similar line that Soloviev develops his argument. 'Faith' alone is an existential or 'substantial' principle; it establishes link and contact with true reality. And yet it needs a 'rational' elaboration, otherwise its experience remains, as it were, not organized. 'Faith' has an obvious existential priority; it gives the true assurance of existence, but it is the 'reason' alone which can give a coherent account of the apprehended reality. Our comparison with Bergson is legitimate, because Soloviev uses the concept of 'faith' in a very wide sense, in which it denotes almost the same basic 'insight' into existence as the 'intuition' of Bergson. In fact, for Soloviev, faith is an integral element of any act of knowledge. 'Faith' (intellectual) 'imagination', and 'realization' (in sensual images) are for him 'fundamental elements of any objective knowledge'.[91]

As commentary, this was entirely apt.

Florovsky wrote elsewhere on the two 'wisdoms' involved.

Soloviev has often been accused of pantheism. But it is not in this that the *proton pseudon* [primary falsehood] of his religious and philosophical system lies. The boundary between the eternal, the anarchistic and created, between the absolute and final was never erased in his consciousness; and he frequently, even with exaggeration, emphasized the opposition of these principles. The basic flaw of his world view is in something else, in the complete *lack of tragedy* in his religious perception of life. He perceived sin too narrowly, only within his mind, and it did not seem necessary to break the continuity of the natural order of nature in order to overcome it. The world was imagined by him in the form of an ideally constructed mechanism, steadily and precisely

> obeying irreproachable laws given by the Almighty and Wise Creator. This is why he was so attracted by the evolutionary hypothesis, and he applied it to prove the Resurrection of Christ, *his necessity, and consequently his reality*. Indeed, 'nature awaits and languishes for him'. The moral dualism of Good and Evil was perceived by him too abstractly; he did not feel the reality of the 'ideal of Sodom'. Temptations and seductions seemed to him only necessary moments of the realization of freedom, the irresistibility of which for him was provided by reason of the existing, eternal will of God. And living, concrete human personalities disappeared in the face of the inevitable triumph of the general transformation, and all attention was drawn away to the side of abstract forms of social and cosmic being.[92]

These sweeping statements altogether fail to do justice to Solov'ëv's sharply critical comments on political, social and religious institutions, not excluding individual agents.

But of course Florovsky realized that a judgment of ungrounded cosmic optimism could not be the last word on Solov'ëv's career.

> In his last years he passed through a difficult religious crisis, in the purging fire of which all his Gnostic and theocratic utopias burned. He felt not only the sharpness of the sinful sting in the individual soul but also the reality, the independence of evil as a cosmic principle. He felt the catastrophic pulse of history, and instead of the here-and-now Kingdom he saw 'the end of history'—the Last Judgment and the second coming of Christ. 'All great *earthly* matter will dissipate like smoke'—in this discovery his earthly life exploded.[93]

In this same context, Florovsky was unable to resist returning to the topic of a more impressive disciple of Solov'ëv than Anna Shmidt— Sergeï Bulgakov who at one point, ill-advisedly, had encouraged her.[94] Florovsky knew that Bulgakov's intellectual debts were owed at least as much to the monuments of Orthodox tradition as they were to philosophical sources, even if the 'monuments' were accessed at times only via the 'sources' in question.[95] 'Bulgakov's typical problematic of religious or ecclesiastical culture and Christian construction in history were linked to Soloviev, and from there the path led back to Schelling, the Neoplatonists, and also the fathers and the experience of the Great Church—the Church of history, tradition, and patristics.'[96] He makes the (perfectly fair) comment that the influence on Bulgakov of Kantian transcendentalism is unmistakable in the 'very religious-philosophical problem posed in the *Unfading Light*, "How is religion possible?"' He then goes on to claim, much more controversially, that the 'power of German philosophy is also evident in Bulgakov's limited romantic horizon, in his religious *Naturphilosophie*, and in his unrestrained lurch towards the "philosophy of identity" [i.e., where the identity of being and thinking can be established from the side either of nature or of spirit].'[97] But then Florovsky makes an astounding admission. 'Yet Bulgakov confidently returned from religious philosophy to theology, and this provided him with an historical advantage and filial freedom.'[98]

Here Florovsky admits that Bulgakov became ever more acceptable—or, at the least, less unacceptable—to his premier critic in the course of a movement from religious philosopher to dogmatician. Bulgakov's *Unfading Light*, the only major work of directly religious import by which he was known at the time he left the Soviet Union, lies somewhere between an extended essay on the philosophy of religion and a study of philosophical theology. Still strongly under the influence of Solov'ëv, it remained the book by which other Russian Orthodox were likely to judge him in the 1920s and even into the 1930s when the Great Trilogy began to appear (the latter's first volume, *Agnets Bozhiĭ*, 'Lamb of God', in 1933, on the cusp of the 'Sophia Affair'). The 'Sophiology Debate' which so concerned the three distinct Russian jurisdictions of the Inter-war years—the Moscow patriarchate, the Synodal Church or Russian Church in Exile, and the Russian Exarchate of the Patriarchate of Constantinople—would not have taken so acrimonious a form, one hazards, had the specifically dogmatic writings of Bulgakov received an evaluation free of the influence of on *Unfading Light* on readers' minds. For by 1926, at any rate, Bulgakov had become rather more critical in his attitude to Solov'ëv's corpus.[99] Florovsky did not publicly support the anathematizers, though neither would he sign the very gentle critique of Bulgakov's Exarchate colleagues. Privately, he wrote of the 'sophianic heresy'.[100]

Yet even in *Unfading Light* not everything was in some way controversial or problematic. Florovsky might have noted that Bulgakov's Preface, in *Unfading Light*, goes out of its way to attack modern German religious thought for its immanentism and quasi-pantheism (though Schelling is excepted from these strictures). Bulgakov takes a stand there against the inflated pretensions of 'gnosis' of every esoteric kind. At the same time, he also sets his face against world denial. So the task is how to know God in the world and the world in God.

> The distance between the world and God is absolute and insurmountable for the world. If it is overcome, then it is so only exceptionally, by interruption, freely, miraculously, and by grace. Any immanence of the Transcendence, the touch of Divinity, is an act truly miraculous and free, an act of mercy and love, but not an act of law and necessity. God, as the Transcendent, is infinitely, absolutely remote from and alien to the world; there are not and cannot be any naturally determined, methodical paths to him, but precisely therefore he in his condescension becomes infinitely close to us, is the most close, most intimate, most interior, most immanent in us, is found to be closer to us than we are to ourselves. Therefore there is not and cannot be any 'spiritual knowledge' that leans on *method* for cognition of God (and not only of the divine alone). For before absolute distance, in the face of infinity every finite value and path is annihilated: God can send his angel to Balaam's ass, singe an accursed sinner with the fire and light of his appearance; he can overtake his persecutor on the road to Damascus and nevertheless remain inaccessible to the most methodical efforts. For God is Wonder and Freedom, while all knowledge is method and necessity.[101]

One notes how Bulgakov goes on by underlining as a caveat the highly Florovskian notion of *podvig* (though the term also occurs, as mentioned above, in Solov'ëv's writing as well). 'By putting it this way we are denying only that a vision of God comes without fail and in conformity with laws for those who seek him. But the quest for God, the preparation of the self, the disclosure of the divine in the self is accomplished by human effort which God expects of us—"the kingdom of God is compelled by force". The whole of asceticism attests to this.'[102] 'The logic of religious consciousness demands that God be found as the unconditional not-world and the world as the unconditional not-God in order then to see the world in God and God in the world.'[103] Like Solov'ëv, Bulgakov found Hellenism providential and still necessary today, yet it is also philosophically insufficient—as the Idealist idiom of this citation attests.

Florovsky remained adamantly unconvinced of the need for intellectual supplementation from without. 'The Christian Hellenism of the Fathers was a trans-cultural norm, admitting of no translation into the categories of modern philosophy. Not only the content, but also the form of the patristic doctrine of God was an unchangeable *philosophia perennis*.'[104] In any case, 'Faith is kept indivisible in the depths and innermost recesses of church experience. In its inner thoughts on God, its rule of prayer, and its spiritual exploits the Russian soul preserves an ancient and strict patristic style and lives in the full, unpolluted, and indivisible plenitude of *sobornost*'. Too often, however, thought has been torn from its sources, and the first people to return to thought, in the consciousness of their rootlessness, did so too late. "Obscurantism" was a dialectical precaution against such rootlessness. It could be overcome only by creative theological thought, and only when it returned to the depths of the life of the Church and was illuminated from within. When the mind will be contained in the heart, and the heart will see that which the mind contemplates, then there will be an entry into the understanding of truth.'[105]

The emphasis on creativity in theological thought signifies, once again, Florovsky's antipathy to a merely repetitive theology. 'Neo-patristic' does not mean 'archaeological'. 'One must be steeped in the inspiration of the patristic flame and not simply be a gardener pottering around amongst ancient texts... One can follow in the path of the fathers only through creativity, not through imitation.'[106] But the creativity is inaccessible without the *ressourcement*. But who is to judge what degree or quality of 'return to the sources' qualifies the practitioner to set out on theological creation? Solov'ëv had appealed to the Novgorod icons in an apologia for Sophia, and Bulgakov would write on the holy images much more fully than Florovsky ever did.[107] Yet Florovsky holds up the Russian icon so as to shame them for their infidelity to Greek Christianity. 'The most powerful element in Russian ecclesiastical culture is the Russian icon, and this is so precisely because in iconography the Hellenistic experience was spiritually assimilated and realized in a genuine creative intimacy by the Russian masters.'[108] Admittedly, Florovsky attempted to make the further case that the 'Sophia' iconography of the Novgorod icons was owed to the influence of mediaeval German mysticism.[109]

Florovsky never tired of reiterating the crucial formative role of *tserkovnost'*, 'churchliness'—in which perspective Solov'ëv was liturgically deficient in a manner that could hardly be ascribed to Bulgakov. In his theological writings Bulgakov, who once write that 'theology ought to be drunk from the bottom of the Eucharistic chalice', cites the texts used in worship frequently enough.[110] If Florovsky went further it was along the same road. Only in the *sobornost'* of the Church is 'catholic transfiguration' of individual consciousness possible. Theologizing within the environment of *sobornost'* is the quality that must be re-learned. 'The theologian must learn to discover himself continually within the Church through ascetic trial and self-discipline. One must grow into the Church, live in its mysterious supratemporal and integral tradition, and combine in oneself all the fulness of its revelation and insight. In this and in this alone is there assurance of creative productivity.'[111]

The theologian writing in or for Russia and Russians must be not only patristically-minded but Byzantine in his outlook—Solov'ëv's *bête noire*. 'One cannot say that Russian theology, in its creative development, adequately and attentively experienced either patristics or Byzantinism. That task still remains.'[112]

NOTES

1. Paul L. Gavrilyuk, *Georges Florovsky and the Russian Religious Renaissance* (New York and Oxford: Oxford University Press, 2003), p. 4.
2. *Ibid.*, p. 3.
3. Georges Florovsky, 'The Ways of Russian Theology', in *Aspects of Church History, Collected Works IV* (Belmont, MA: Nordland, 1975), pp. 183–231, and here at pp. 191–2 (originally, 'Les Voies de la théologie russe', *Dieu Vivant*, 13 [1949], pp. 39–62).
4. *Ibid.*, pp. 192–3. Italics original.
5. Smith, *Vladimir Soloviev and the Spiritualization of Matter*, p. 147.
6. Florovsky, 'The Ways of Russian Theology', p. 194.
7. Emphasized in Gavrilyuk, *Georges Florovsky and the Russian Religious Renaissance*, pp. 80–97.
8. *Ibid.*, p. 24. Compare the list of Florovsky's intellectual debts to moderns, in *ibid.*, pp. 260–1.
9. *Ibid.*, p. 38.
10. Cited *ibid.*, p. 39.
11. *Ibid.*
12. Gavrilyuk, *Georges Florovsky and the Russian Religious Renaissance*, p. 222. Florovsky's fundamental theology is accessibly laid out in his essay, 'Revelation and Interpretation', in *Bible, Church, Tradition: An Eastern Orthodox View. Collected Works* I (Belmont, MA: Nordland, 1972), pp. 17–36.
13. Florovsky, 'The Ways of Russian Theology', p. 194. Italics original.
14. Gavrilyuk, *Georges Florovsky and the Russian Religious Renaissance*, pp. 208, 250, 269.
15. Florovsky, 'The Ways of Russian Theology', pp. 195–6. Italics original.
16. Reciprocated in Jewish admiration of this honorary member of the Society for the Spread of Enlightenment among Jews in Russia. See Hamutal bar-Yosef, 'The Jewish Reception of Vladimir Solov'ëv', in van den Bercken, de Courten and van der Zweerde, *Vladimir Solov'ëv*, pp. 363–92.
17. Florovsky, 'The Ways of Russian Theology', p. 196.
18. Georges Florovsky, 'The Fathers of the Church and the Old Testament', in *Aspects of Church History. Collected Works IV*, pp. 31–8 and here at p. 32.
19. Quoted in Smith, *Vladimir Soloviev and the Spiritualization of Matter*, p. 160. See also Walter G. Moss, 'Vladimir Soloviev and the Jews in Russia', *Russian Review*, 29 (1970), pp. 181–91.

20. Florovsky., 'The Ways of Russian Theology', p. 196.
21. *Ibid.*, p. 197.
22. Gavrilyuk, *Georges Florovsky and the Russian Religious Renaissance*, p. 215.
23. Étienne Gilson, *The Elements of Christian Philosophy* (New York, NY: Doubleday, 1960).
24. Florovsky, 'The Ways of Russian Theology', p. 200.
25. *Ibid.*, p. 201.
26. *Ibid.*
27. Sergius Bulgakov, *Sous les remparts de Chersonèse* (Geneva: Ad Solem, 1999).
28. Florovsky, 'The Ways of Russian Theology', p. 202. Italics original.
29. Karl Barth, *Ad limina apostolorum. An appraisal of Vatican II* (Edinburgh: St Andrew's Press, 1969).
30. Florovsky, 'The Ways of Russian Theology', p. 204.
31. Georges Florovsky, *The Ways of Russian Theology, Part One. Collected Works*, V (Belmont, MA: Nordland, 1979), p. xvii.
32. *Ibid.*, p. xviii.
33. Gavrilyuk, *Georges Florovsky and the Russian Religious Renaissance*, p. 66.
34. Marlène Laruelle, *Russian Eurasianism: An Ideology of Empire* (Baltimore, MD: Johns Hopkins Press, 2008).
35. Florovsky, *The Ways of Russian Theology, Part Two*, p. 152.
36. Russian 'love of wisdom' (*lyubomudrie*) had its beginning precisely in the ecclesiastical schools', 'the foundations for systematic philosophical culture were laid in the ecclesiastical schools', *The Ways of Russian Theology, Part Two. Collected Works*, VI (Vaduz: Büchervertriebsanstalt, 1987), p. 9.
37. *Ibid.*, p. 11.
38. *Ibid.*
39. T. E. Hulme, *Speculations. Essays on Humanism and the Philosophy of Art* (London: Kegan Paul, 1936), p. 118.
40. Florovsky, *The Ways of Russian Theology, Part Two*, p. 265.
41. *Ibid.*, p. 275. Compare Nicolas Zernov, *The Russian Religious Renaissance of the Twentieth Century* (London: Darton, Longman and Todd, 1963).
42. Florovsky, *The Ways of Russian Theology, Part Two*, p. 275.
43. *Ibid.*
44. *Ibid.*
45. *Ibid.*

46. *Ibid.*, p. 276.
47. Sergius Bulgakov, 'Osnovnye problem teorii progressa', in his *Problemÿ idealizma* (Moscow: Modest Kolerov i 'Tre Kvadrata', 2002 [1902]), p. 287, cited in Gavrilyuk, *Georges Florovsky and the Russian Religious Renaissance*, p. 17.
48. See Bernice Glatzer Rosenthal, 'The Nature and Function of Sophia in Sergeï Bulgakov's Prerevolutionary Thought', in Deutsch Kornblatt and Gustafson, *Russian Religious Thought*, pp. 154–75.
49. Natalino Valentini, *Volti dell'anima russa. Identità culturale e spirituale del cristianesimo slavo-ortodosso* (Milan: Edizione Paoline, 2012).
50. Georges Florovsky, 'Western Influences in Russian Theology', in *Aspects of Church History*, pp. 157–82, and here at pp. 176–7.
51. Florovsky, *The Ways of Russian Theology*, Part Two, p. 79.
52. *Ibid.*, pp. 79–80.
53. *Ibid.*, p. 80.
54. *Ibid.*
55. *Ibid.*
56. *Ibid.*, pp. 80–1.
57. *Ibid.*, p. 81.
58. *Ibid.*, p. 82.
59. *Ibid.*, p. 85.
60. *Ibid.*, p. 86.
61. *Ibid.*
62. *Ibid.*
63. *Ibid.*
64. *Ibid.*
65. *Ibid.*
66. Brandon Gallaher, 'The Christological Focus of Vladimir Solov'ev's Sophiology', *Modern Theology*, 25. 4 (2009), pp. 617–46.
67. van den Bercken, 'The Macrochristianity of Vladimir Solov'ëv', p. 65.
68. *Ibid.*
69. *Ibid.*, p. 69.
70. Florovsky, *The Ways of Russian Theology*, Part Two, p. 87.
71. *Ibid.*
72. *Lectures on Godmanhood*, p. 192.
73. *Ibid.*, p. 195.

74. *Ibid.*, p. 196.
75. *Ibid.*
76. Andrew Louth, 'Is Development of Doctrine a Valid Category for Orthodox Theology?', in Valerie Hotchkiss and Patrick Henry (eds.), *Orthodoxy and Western Culture* (Westchester, NY: St Vladimir's Seminary Press, 2005), pp. 45–63. In a paper read to Karl Barth's theological seminar at Bonn in 1931, Florovsky repudiated the phrase 'development of dogma', for 'dogmas do not develop; they are unchanging and inviolable, even in their external aspect - their wording ... Dogma is an intuitive truth, not a discursive axiom which is accessible to logical development', 'Revelation, Philosophy and Theology', in Georges Florovsky, *Creation and Redemption. Collected Works, III* (Belmont, MA: Nordland, 1976), pp. 21–42, and here at p. 30.
77. Florovsky, *The Ways of Russian Theology, Part Two*, p. 156.
78. *Ibid.*
79. *Ibid.*
80. *Ibid.*, p. 157.
81. *Ibid.*, p. 158.
82. *Ibid.*, p. 161.
83. *Ibid.*, p. 245.
84. *Ibid.*
85. *Ibid.*, p. 250.
86. *Ibid.*, p. 251.
87. *Ibid.*, p. 253.
88. Georges Florovsky, 'Reason and Faith in the Philosophy of Solov'ev', in Ernest J. Simmons (ed.), *Continuity and Change in Russian and Soviet Thought* (Cambridge, MA: Harvard University Press, 1955), pp. 283–97.
89. *Ibid.*, p. 284.
90. *Ibid.*
91. *Ibid.*, p. 286, with an internal citation of Henri Bergson, *Creative Intuition* (New York, 1944), pp. 166–7, and, subsequently, of Solov'ëv's *Kritika otvlechennykh nachal*, in the collected works at *Socheneniia*, II, pp. 342ff.
92. Georges Florovsky, 'Human Wisdom and the Great Wisdom of God', in *Philosophy. Philosophical Problems and Movements. Collected Works* XII (Vaduz: Büchervertriebsanstalt, 1989), pp. 110–21, and here at pp. 112–13.
93. *Ibid.*, p. 113.
94. Solov'ëv had thought her mentally ill, so it was extremely foolish of Bulgakov, aided and abetted by Florensky, to publish her theosophical musings in 1916. See Gavrilyuk, *Georges Florovsky and the Russian Religious*

Renaissance, p. 117. Bulgakov later repented of this action which had poured oil on the flames of Florovsky's growing distrust of Solov'ëv, *ibid.*, p. 118.

95. For Florovsky's relations with Bulgakov, see *ibid.*, pp. 114–31; for Florovsky's covert opposition to Bulgakov's theological approach, see *ibid.*, pp. 132–58: 'Florovsky's historical theology was shaped by his polemical reaction to sophiology', *ibid.*, p. 133.
96. Florovsky, *The Ways of Russian Theology, Part Two*, p. 113.
97. *Ibid.*
98. *Ibid.*
99. Gavrilyuk, *Georges Florovsky and the Russian Religious Renaissance*, p. 118, n. 17.
100. *Ibid.*, p. 140, n. 25.
101. Sergius Bulgakov, *Unfading Light. Contemplations and Speculations* (Grand Rapids, MI: Eerdmans, 2012), pp. 22–3.
102. *Ibid.*, p. 23.
103. *Ibid.*
104. Gavrilyuk, *Georges Florovsky and the Russian Religious Renaissance*, p. 204.
105. Florovsky, *The Ways of Russian Theology, Part Two*, p. 293.
106. *Ibid.*, p. 294.
107. Sergius Bulgakov, *Ikona i ikonopochitanie* (Paris: YMCA, 1931); there is an English translation in *Icons and the Name of God* (Grand Rapids, MI: Eerdmans, 2012), pp. 1–114; compare Georges Florovsky, 'Holy Ikons', in *Creation and Redemption. Collected Works III* (Belmont, MA: Nordland, 1976), pp. 209–12.
108. Florovsky, *The Ways of Russian Theology, Part Two*, p. 297.
109. Gavrilyuk, *Georges Florovsky and the Russian Religious Renaissance*, p. 143.
110. Cited *ibid.*, p. 119.
111. Florovsky, *The Ways of Russian Theology, Part Two*, p. 295.
112. *Ibid.*, pp. 296–7.

Conclusion

In December 1925 Florovsky wrote to Bulgakov,

> By renouncing Solovyov we will be liberated from the whole shadowy tradition, which leads from Masonry to the extra-ecclesial mysticism of the false contemplatives in bad taste. I feel that it is this tradition that has held our creative forces in shackles. We must enter anew 'the Father's house' divested of worldly wisdom and then be armed anew with the new wealth and medicine of grace. As for Solovyov, instead of singing him panegyrics or even hymns of praise, we should instead offer prayers for his troubled and half-broken soul.[1]

Thirty years later, irritated that people still cited his first ever published article—an enthusiastic acclamation of Solov'ëv's primacy in Russian philosophy from 1912—Florovsky formally retracted the praise he had lavished then.[2]

His anxieties, and those of the other critics of sophiology, in the Orthodox Church and elsewhere, remain alive today. German Idealism—undoubtedly an influence on Solov'ëv—leads directly, so it is said, to a pantheistic, and thus heterodox, view of the world.

> 'Idealism becomes pantheism.' Despite all its inaccuracy, this name conceived afterwards, indicates rightly the basic tendency of German Idealism... The basic idea of pantheism is the absolute, insoluble connection of God with the world, the idea of mutual closest connection. In the recognition of 'reciprocity' lies the acuteness of pantheism. For pantheism recognizes not only the foundation of the world in God, but

also claims that God absolutely needs the world, that he has to reveal himself in it, that his existence in the world—and thereby the world itself—constitutively belongs to the perfection of the divine existence. This conclusion is drawn in order to explain the world. Otherwise, the existence of the world would be completely senseless, an additional accident could disturb its harmony. Moreover, nothing unnecessary, nothing changeable, can be added to something absolute, for then this perfection itself would be disturbed. Considered that way, the world becomes the eternal double of God. The world cannot be non-existent, because then God would not exist either, but then God would not be God. If the world did not have to exist, it would not exist; for nothing can be added to divine perfection from without. Consequently, the world is an eternal self-revelation of God, an eternal changing existence of divine life.[3]

One obvious question to ask is whether this hat fits the sophiologists' heads. Writing in 1923 in the Prague journal *Russkaya mÿsl'*, Florovsky had no doubt. Solov'ëv's 'panentheism was indistinguishable from pantheism.'[4] Still, in *The Ways of Russian Theology* Florovsky would give Solov'ëv a bill of doctrinal health in the matter. Yet the 'metaxological' role of Sophia may suggest to any reader some degree of hesitation on that score. Does God create out of nothing, or out of 'the eternal divine world that pre-exists temporal creation'[5]? One might answer, 'Both, in different senses', but the matter clearly requires discussion—which Florovsky indeed gave it in regard to Bulgakov, while nonetheless, for reasons of academic diplomacy, naming no names.

Vseedinstvo was also a neuralgic concept. In 'The Crisis of German Idealism', Florovsky had launched a frontal attack. 'One can speak of the aesthetic determinism of Idealist philosophy. It is already determined in advance by the theory of the world as an organic and complete whole. Idealism does not permit any gaps or unevenness in existence. It believes in the adjustment of all faults and imperfections.'[6] Florovsky's criticism of the *vseedinstvo* idea as an invitation to Voltairean sarcasm—all is for the best in the best of all possible worlds—had implications for the question of the historical process and its meaning, as he was not slow to point out. For the Idealist, 'The meaning of history, which lies beyond time, consists in this appearance and emergence of the prototypes in concrete forms ... But the Idealist denial of history has still another pole: actual meaning can only reveal itself in the whole.'[7] Florovsky had already deplored the insufficient sense of tragedy in Solov'ëv's view of humanity (at any rate, until the last year of his life). He could also find, at least implicitly, a closure to comedy as well—since in Idealism there can be no absolute novelty, and hence no true drama, even one with a happy ending. 'For the Idealists, development is a morphological concept, not a dynamic one. Development is a revelation; there is nothing creative about it. Nothing is created anew. Development is revelation of form. A theory of development is always a theory of preformation. That is why development can always be rationally calculated and determined beforehand.'[8] It should be borne in mind that Florovsky's own philosophy of history has been deemed, for much of his life, a-teleological in character—extraordinarily so for someone schooled in biblical eschatology. 'History leads nowhere' is a summary of 'epistemic agnosticism about history's ultimate purposes' which sounds distinctly odd when ascribed to a Christian theologian.[9]

Moreover, Florovsky inferred from the controlling intuition of *vseedinstvo* a depreciation, if not a denial, of special revelation—no place here for the uniqueness of the biblical trajectory of experience and reflection.

> The small and insignificant feeling for the historical leads Idealism to a strange Docetism in the reception and interpretation of Christianity. In accordance with its nature, Idealism tends to deny *Revelation* completely. From its point of view, *everything* is revelation. That is why revelation disappears in history, dissolves in historical continuity. The generality of the revelation renders impossible special unique revelations. In Idealism revelation changes from

an elementary rupture from another world to a stage of development.[10]

Such a view of revelation might well be coupled, he thought, with an excessively allegorical approach to revelation's record in Scripture. 'The Idealists regard revelation as the appearance and emergence of divine potencies or of the foundations of the world. With this, revelation takes on a symbolical character. For the Idealists the meaning of revelation is to name the ideal and to point towards it. This is connected with the tendency for a symbolic reception and interpretation of the Bible.'[11] And Florovsky went so far as to speak of 'the decomposition of history into symbols, which is the exclusion of time.'[12] But does Solov'ëv's cosmology, seen as an account of nature and history, correspond to this Idealist image? Ironically, Solov'ëv's debt to Schelling accentuated rather than diminished his sense of both cosmic evolution and salvation history (not for nothing did specifically Russian interest in Schelling tick those particular boxes). Does Solov'ëv's exegesis downplay the historically concrete character of the biblical narrative in favour of a Symbolist aesthetic? It would have been impossible to ascribe to the Incarnation, the Temptations, the Passion and the Resurrection of Christ all that Solov'ëv actually does had he adopted an a-temporal 'symbology'.

What of 'God-manhood'? 'German Idealism could never acknowledge, could never comprehend, that the fate of man could be determined in empirical time. That is why it could neither perceive nor acknowledge the historical God-man. One could say that German Idealism is a theory of God-humanity without the God-man.'[13] Would it be true to say of Solov'ëv that the principle of God-manhood meant more to him than Christ, the God-man? As noted above, if there was any doubt on that score before the writing of *The Legend of the Antichrist* there could be none afterwards.

For Florovsky, German influence was toxic for Russian thought because Protestantism (and for late-nineteenth- and early-twentieth-century European commentators Germany was *par excellence* the Protestant nation), in its rejection of the *philosophia Christiana*, made possible the revival in the German

Conclusion

philosophical tradition of a pre-Christian Hellenism,[14] untouched by the regenerative influence of the Church Fathers. Could it be said of Solov'ëv's thought, or indeed Bulgakov's, that they had returned to a Hellenic philosophy unshaped by specifically Christian categories? The concept which best fits Florovsky's criticism is that of the 'world soul', variously and ambivalently related to 'Sophia' as that concept is in Solov'ëv's work. The 'world soul' was an element in ancient philosophy the Fathers declined to embrace. Christians of the sub-apostolic and patristic eras 'avoided reference to the World Soul', fearing its 'associations with sympathetic magic and the occult', and confident of its cosmological superfluity.[15] 'Such a soul played no significant role in the theological work of the early Christians.'[16] With good reason, the part (or parts) played by the world soul has been called a 'structural deficiency' in Solov'ëv's thought, 'unfounded' and 'ultimately untenable', marring a cosmology that is otherwise not only Christianity-compatible but internally coherent.[17] In the words of Father Robert Slesinski,

> While one can argue for consistency between a Divine Sophia or Wisdom of God conceived as the complexus of Ideas or Exemplars in the Divine Mind (although ultimately there can only be one Form of forms and one Truth of truths), and then as creatural Sophia manifested finitely in the universe as an image and resplendence of God's being, one cannot do the same for Sophia as an *intermediary* world soul with a will of her own whose vocation (when she is not self-willed, as it were) is somehow to unite God with his creation or promote a harmonious blend between heavenly Sophia and her earthly counterpart.[18]

Slesinksi defends the twofold Wisdom theme, and it is indeed defensible without losing Florovsky's 'intuition of creaturehood' for it respects the Creator/creature divide. But let us give Solov'ëv's premier theological disciple the last word on Sophia, and thus, by implication, on 'The Sophiology Man'. On 31 December 1928, Bulgakov wrote:

> Sophia, the Wisdom of God, is the revelation of the life of the Trinitarian God, the manifestation of the nature of the Divinity, and in this sense the Glory of God. Sophia belongs to the entire Trinity as the self-revelation of the Divinity. Sophia has no proper hypostatic being, but is hypostatized in each of the divine Hypostases. As divine life *in actu* Sophia is an energy unveiling the divine *ousia* or essence of God and manifesting itself in the world as the hidden and unveiled depth of the divine life, its strength and its idea. Sophia, the energy, is God but not in the sense of the subject but in that of the complement (not *ho Theos*, in Greek, but *theios*). God creates the world by his Wisdom or in his Wisdom.[19]

'Glory', 'hypostasis', 'energy' and 'essence', 'unveiling' (revelation), 'creation'—what is this if not the vocabulary the Fathers drew from their sources, whether biblical or philosophical, and which, reshaped, they transmitted to the Byzantine theologians and the wider Church?

NOTES

1. Cited in Gavrilyuk, *Georges Florovsky and the Russian Religious Renaissance*, p. 98.
2. Florovsky, 'Reason and Faith in the Philosophy of Solov'ev', p. 297.
3. Georges Florovsky, 'The Crisis of German Idealism, I. The "Hellenism" of German Idealism', in *Collected Works XII, Philosophy. Philosophical Problems and Movements*, pp. 23–30, and here at p. 27.
4. Cited in Gavrilyuk, *Georges Florovsky and the Russian Religious Renaissance*, p. 105. On the character of panentheism, see John W. Cooper, *Panentheism. The Other God of the Philosophers: From Plato to the Present* (Grand Rapids, MI: Baker Academic, 2006), where the crucial distinction is made between a panentheism where the world can affect God and one where it cannot. Solov'ëv's version seems to fall into the latter category.
5. Gavrilyuk, *Georges Florovsky and the Russian Religious Renaissance*, p. 146.
6. Florovsky, 'The Crisis of German Idealism', p. 28.
7. Georges Florovsky, 'The Crisis of German Idealism, II. The Crisis of Idealism as the Crisis of Reformation', in *Collected Works XII, Philosophy. Philosophical Problems and Movements*, pp. 31–41, and here at p. 33.

8. *Ibid.*, p. 34.
9. Gavrilyuk, *Georges Florovsky and the Russian Religious Renaissance*, pp. 168, 86. Gavrilyuk considers that Florovsky had abandoned such a-teleology by 1959, the date of his essay 'The Predicament of the Christian Historian', in *Christianity and Culture. Collected Works II* (Belmont, MA: Nordland, 1976), pp. 31–66.
10. Georges Florovsky, 'The Crisis of German Idealism, II', p. 35.
11. *Ibid.*, p. 36.
12. *Ibid.*
13. *Ibid.*, p. 38.
14. *Ibid.*, p. 40.
15. Wendy Elgersma Helleman, 'The World Soul and Sophia', in van den Bercken, de Courten and van der Zweerde, *Vladimir Solov'ëv*, pp. 163–84, and here at p. 182.
16. *Ibid.*
17. Robert Slesinski, 'Sophiology as a Metaphysics of Creation according to V. S. Solov'ëv', *ibid.*, pp. 131–45, and here at pp. 145, 144.
18. *Ibid.*, p. 141.
19. Nikita Struve and T. Emelianova, *Bratstvo svyatoĭ Sofii, materialÿ i dokumentÿ, 1923–1939* (Paris: YMCA Press, 2000), p. 142.

BIBLIOGRAPHY

Arjakovsky, Antoine, 'The Sophiology of Father Sergii Bulgakov and Contemporary Western Theology', *Saint Vladimir's Theology Quarterly* 49.1–2 (2005), pp. 219–35

Balthasar, Hans Urs von, *Cosmic Liturgy. The Universe according to Maximus the Confessor* (San Francisco: Ignatius, 2003)

—— 'Soloviev', in *The Glory of the Lord. A Theological Aesthetics, III. Studies in Theological Styles: Lay Styles* (Edinburgh: T. & T. Clark, 1986), pp. 279–352

Bar-Yosef, Hamutal, 'The Jewish Reception of Vladimir Solov'ëv', in van den Bercken, de Courten and van der Zweerde, *Vladimir Solov'ëv*, pp. 363–92

Bercken, Wil van den, 'The Macrochristianity of Vladimir Solov'ëv. A Collectivist and Geographical Concept of Christian Religion', in van den Bercken, de Courten and van der Zweerde, *Vladimir Solov'ëv*, pp. 64–84

Bercken, Wil van den, Manon de Courten and Evert van der Zweerde (eds.), *Vladimir Solov'ëv: Reconciler and Polemicist* (Leuven: Peeters, 2000)

Barth Karl, *Ad limina apostolorum. An Appraisal of Vatican II* (Edinburgh: St Andrew's Press, 1969)

Bouyer, Louis, *The Church of God. Body of Christ and Temple of the Spirit* (San Francisco: Ignatius Press, 2011)

—— *Cosmos. The World and the Glory of God* (Petersham, MA: St Bede's Press, 1988)

Bulgakov, Sergius [Sergeï], *Ikona i ikonopochitanie* (Paris: YMCA, 1931); English translation, *Icons and the Name of God* (Grand Rapids, MI: Eerdmans, 2012), pp. 1–114

—— *The Lamb of God* (Grand Rapids, MI: Eerdmans, 2008)

Bulgakov, Sergius, *Sous les remparts de Chersonèse* (Geneva: Ad Solem, 1999)

—— *Unfading Light. Contemplations and Speculations* (Grand Rapids, MI: Eerdmans, 2012)

—— *The Wisdom of God. A Brief Summary of Sophiology* (New York and London: Williams & Norgate, 1937)

Burrell, David B., 'Act of Creation with its Theological Consequences', in Thomas Weinandy, Daniel Keating, John Yocum (eds.), *Aquinas on Doctrine. A Critical Introduction* (London and New York: T. & T. Clark, 2004), pp. 27–44

Carlson, Maria, *'No Religion Higher than Truth': A History of the Theosophical Movement in Russia, 1875–1922* (Princeton, NJ: Princeton University Press, 1993)

Cioran, Samuel D., *Vladimir Solov'ev and the Knighthood of the Divine Sophia* (Waterloo, Ontario: Wilfrid Laurier University Press, 1977)

Cooper, John W., *Panentheism. The Other God of the Philosophers: From Plato to the Present* (Grand Rapids, MI: Baker Academic, 2006)

Copleston, Frederick, SJ, *Philosophy in Russia. From Herzen to Lenin and Berdyaev* (Tunbridge Wells: Search Press, 1986)

Courten, Manon de, *History, Sophia and the Russian Newman* (Berne: Peter Lang, 2004)

David, Zdenek V., 'The Influence of Jakob Boehme on Russian Religious Thought', *Slavic Review* 21. 1 (1962), pp. 43–64

Desmond, William, 'God beyond the Whole: Between Solov'ëv and Shestov', in his *Is there a Sabbath for Thought? Between Religion and Philosophy* (New York: Fordham University Press, 2005), pp. 167–99

Deutsch Kornblatt, Judith (ed.), *Divine Sophia: The Wisdom Writings of Vladimir Solovyov* (Ithaca, NY: Cornell University Press, 2009)

—— and Richard F. Gustafson (eds.), *Russian Religious Thought* (Madison, WI: University of Wisconsin Press, 1996)

Dostoevsky, Thedor Mikhailovitch, *The Brothers Karamazov* (London: J. M. Dent, 1927)

Emery, Gilles, 'The Doctrine of the Trinity in St Thomas Aquinas', in Thomas Weinandy, Daniel Keating and John Yocum (eds.), *Aquinas on Doctrine. A Critical Introduction* (London and New York: T. & T. Clark, 2004), pp. 45–66

Fabro, Cornelio, *Participation et causalité selon S. Thomas d'Aquin* (Louvain: Publications universitaires de Louvain, 1961)

Florovsky, Georges, 'The Crisis of German Idealism, I. The "Hellenism" of German Idealism', in *Philosophy. Philosophical Problems and Movements. Collected Works XII* (Vaduz: Büchervertriebsanstalt, 1989), pp. 23–30

—— 'The Crisis of German Idealism, II. The Crisis of Idealism as the Crisis of Reformation', in *Philosophy. Philosophical Problems and Movements. Collected Works XII* (Vaduz: Büchervertriebsanstalt, 1989), pp. 31–41

—— 'The Fathers of the Church and the Old Testament', in *Aspects of Church History. Collected Works IV* (Belmont, MA: Nordland, 1975), pp. 31–8

—— 'Holy Ikons', in *Creation and Redemption. Collected Works III* (Belmont, MA: Nordland, 1976), pp. 209–12

—— 'Human Wisdom and the Great Wisdom of God', in *Philosophy. Philosophical Problems and Movements. Collected Works XII* (Vaduz: Büchervertriebsanstalt, 1989), pp. 110–21

—— 'The Predicament of the Christian Historian', in *Christianity and Culture. Collected Works II* (Belmont, MA: Nordland, 1976), pp. 31–66

—— 'Reason and Faith in the Philosophy of Solov'ev', in Ernest J. Simmons (ed.), *Continuity and Change in Russian and Soviet Thought* (Cambridge, MA: Harvard University Press, 1955), pp. 283–97

—— 'Revelation and Interpretation', in *Bible, Church, Tradition: An Eastern Orthodox View. Collected Works I* (Belmont, MA: Nordland, 1972), pp. 17–36

—— 'Revelation, Philosophy and Theology', in *Creation and Redemption. Collected Works III* (Belmont, MA: Nordland, 1976), pp. 21–42

—— *The Ways of Russian Theology, Part One. Collected Works V.* (Belmont, MA: Nordland, 1979)

—— *The Ways of Russian Theology, Part Two. Collected Works VI* (Vaduz: Büchervertriebsanstalt, 1987)

—— 'The Ways of Russian Theology', in *Aspects of Church History. Collected Works IV* (Belmont, MA: Nordland, 1975), pp. 183–231

—— 'Western Influences in Russian Theology', in *Aspects of Church*

History. Collected Works IV (Belmont, MA: Nordland, 1975), pp. 157–82

Frank, S. L. (ed.), *A Solovyov Anthology* (London: SCM Press, 1950)

Gallaher, Brandon, 'Antinomism, Trinity and the Challenge of Solov'ëvan Pantheism in the Theology of Sergij Bulgakov', *Studies in Eastern European Thought* 64 (2012), pp. 202–25

——'The Christological Focus of Vladimir Solov'ev's Sophiology', *Modern Theology* 25. 4 (2009), pp. 617–46

Gavrilyuk, Paul L., *Georges Florovsky and the Russian Religious Renaissance* (New York and Oxford: Oxford University Press, 2013)

Gilby, Thomas, OP, *St Thomas Aquinas*, Summa theologiae, 8. *Creation, Variety and Evil [Ia.44–9]* (London: Blackfriars, 1967)

Gilson, Étienne, *The Elements of Christian Philosophy* (New York: Doubleday, 1960)

——*L'Ésprit de la philosophie médiévale* (Paris: Vrin, 1960)

Gleason, Abbott, *European and Muscovite: Ivan Kireevsky and the Origins of Slavophilism* (Cambridge, MA: Harvard University Press, 1972)

Helleman, Wendy Elgersma, *Solovyov's* Sophia *as a Nineteenth Century Russian Appropriation of Dante's Beatrice* (Lewiston, NY: Edwin Mellen Press, 2010)

Herman, Maxime, *Vie et œuvre de Vladimir Soloviev* (Fribourg: Éditions universitaires, 1995 [1947])

Hulme, T. E., *Speculations. Essays on Humanism and the Philosophy of Art* (London: Kegan Paul, 1936)

Kireevsky, Ivan V., 'On the Nature of European Culture and its Relation to the Culture of Russia', in Marc Raeff (ed.), *Russian Intellectual History. An Anthology* (Atlantic Highlands, NJ: Humanities Press, 1978 [1966]), pp. 175–207

——'On the Necessity and Possibility of New Principles in Philosophy', in Peter K. Christoff, *An Introduction to Nineteenth Century Russian Slavophilism, II. I. V. Kireevkij* (The Hague: Mouton, 1972), pp. 346–75

Kostalevsky, Marina, *Dostoevsky and Soloviev: The Art of Integral Vision* (New Haven, CT, and London: Yale University Press, 1997)

Laruelle, Marlène, *Russian Eurasianism: An Ideology of Empire* (Baltimore, MD: Johns Hopkins University Press, 2008)

Lemna, Keith, *The Apocalypse of Wisdom. Louis Bouyer's Theological Recovery of the Cosmos* (Brooklyn, NY: Angelico Press, 2019)

Lossky, Vladimir, and Nicolas Arseniev, *La Paternité spirituelle en Russie au XVIIIème et XIXème siecles* (Bellefontaine: Abbaye de Bellefontaine, 1977)

Louth, Andrew, 'Is Development of Doctrine a Valid Category for Orthodox Theology?', in Valerie Hotchkiss and Patrick Henry (eds.), *Orthodoxy and Western Culture* (Westchester, NY: St Vladimir's Seminary Press, 2005), pp. 45–63

Meerson, Michael Aksionov, 'The Retrieval of Neoplatonism in Solov'ëv's Trinitarian Synthesis', in van den Bercken, de Courten and van der Zweerde, *Vladimir Solov'ëv*, pp. 233–49

Moss, Walter G., 'Vladimir Soloviev and the Jews in Russia', *Russian Review* 29 (1970), pp. 181–91

Nemeth, Thomas, *The Early Solov'ëv and his Quest for Metaphysics* (Cham: Springer, 2004)

—— *The Later Solov'ëv. Philosophy in Imperial Russia* (Cham: Springer, 2019)

—— (ed.), *Vladimir Solov'ëv's Justification of the Moral Good* (Cham: Springer, 2015)

Nichols, Aidan, O. P., 'Solovyov and the Papacy: A Catholic Evaluation', *Communio* XXIV. 1 (1997), pp. 143–59

—— *Wisdom from Above. A Primer in the Theology of Father Sergei Bulgakov* (Leominster: Gracewing, 2005)

Raeff, Marc, 'Enticements and Rifts: Georges Florovsky as Russian Intellectual Historian', in Andrew Blane (ed.), *Georges Florovsky. Russian Intellectual and Orthodox Churchman* (Crestwood, NY: St Vladimir's Seminary Press, 1993), pp. 219–86

Reynolds, Barbara, *Dante. The Poet, the Political Thinker, the Man* (London and New York: I. B. Tauris, 2006)

Ricœur, Paul, *The Symbolism of Evil* (New York, NY: Harper and Row, 1967 [1960])

Riesenfeld, Harald, *The Gospel Tradition* (Philadelphia: Fortress, 1970)

Sagnard, F.-M., *La Gnosie valentienne et le témoignage de saint Irénée* (Paris: Vrin, 1947)

Slesinski, Robert, 'Bulgakov on Sophia', *Journal of Eastern Christian Studies* 59 (2007), pp. 131–45

—— 'Bulgakov's Sophiological Concept of Creation', *Orientalia Christiana Periodica* 74 (2008), pp. 443–54

—— 'Sophiology as a Metaphysics of Creation according to V. S. Solov'ëv', in Wil van den Bercken, Manon de Courten, Evert van der Zweerde (eds.), *Vladimir Solov'ëv: Reconciler and Polemicist* (Leuven: Peeters, 2000), pp. 131–45

Smith, Oliver, *Vladimir Soloviev and the Spiritualization of Matter* (Brighton, MA: Academic Studies Press, 2011)

Soloviev, Sergeï M., *Zhizn' i tvorchestkaya évolyutsiya Vladimira Solov'eva* (Brussels: Zhizn s Bogom, 1997); translations: *Vie de Wladimir Solowiew par son neveu* (Paris: S. O. S., 1982); *Vladimir Soloviev: His Life and Creative Evolution* (Fairfax, VN: Eastern Christian Publications, 2000)

Soloviev, Vladimir, *Crise de la Philosophie occidentale* (Paris: Aubier, 1947)

—— *The Crisis of Western Philosophy: Against the Positivists* (Hudson, NY: Lindisfarne Press, 1996)

—— *Les Fondements spirituels de la vie* (Paris: Beauchesne, 1932)

—— *God, Man and the Church. The Spiritual Foundations of Life* (London: James Clarke, 1938)

—— *Justification of the Moral Good*, ed. Thomas Nemeth (Cham: Springer, 2015)

—— *La Grande Controverse et la politique chrÉtienne [Orient-Occident]* (Paris: Aubier, 1953)

—— *Lectures on Godmanhood* (London: Dennis Dobson, 1948)

—— *The Meaning of Love* (London: Geoffrey Bles, 1945)

—— *The Philosophical Principles of Integral Knowledge* (Grand Rapids, MI: Eerdmans, 2008)

—— *Pisma* (ed.), Ernest L. Radlov (St Petersburg, Obshchestvennaya Pol'za, 1911)

—— *Russia and the Universal Church* (London: Geoffrey Bles, 1948)

—— *Sobranie sochinenii Sobranii Vladimira Sergeevicha Solov'ëva*, ed. Sergeï M. Solov'ëv and Ernest L. Radlov (1st edition, St Petersburg:

Obshchestvennaya Pol'za, 1901–7, 9 volumes; 2nd edition, St Petersburg: Prosveshchenie, 1911–14, 10 volumes), reprinted in the West during the Soviet period, with two additional volumes, consisting chiefly of the correspondence (Brussels: Zhizn' s Bogom, 1966–70)

—— *'La Sophia' et les autres écrits français* (Lausanne: La Cité, 1978)

—— *Trois entretiens sur la guerre, la morale et la religion* (Paris: Plon, 1916)

—— *War, Progress, and the End of History. Three Conversations, including a Short Story of the Anti-Christ* (Hudson, NY: Lindisfarne Press, 1990)

Stead, G. C., 'The Valentinian Myth of Sophia', *Journal of Theological Studies*, New Series 20 (1969), pp. 75–104

Struve, Nikita, and T. Emelianova, *Bratstvo svyatoĭ Sofii, materialÿ i dokumentÿ, 1923–1939* (Paris: YMCA Press, 2000)

Sutton, Jonathan, *The Religious Philosophy of Vladimir Solovyov. Towards a Reassessment* (Basingstoke: Macmillan, 1988)

Tollofsen, Torstein, *The Christocentric Cosmology of St Maximus the Confessor* (Oxford: Oxford University Press, 2008)

Valliere, Paul, *Modern Russian Theology. Bukharev, Soloviev, Bulgakov. Orthodox Theology in a New Key* (Edinburgh: T. & T. Clark, 2000)

—— 'Russian Religious Thought and the Future of Orthodox Theology', *Saint Vladimir's Theological Quarterly* 45 .3 (2001), pp. 227–41

—— 'Solov'ëv and Schelling's Philosophy of Revelation', in Wil van den Bercken, Manon de Courten, Evert van der Zweerde (eds.), *Vladimir Solov'ëv: Reconciler and Polemicist* (Leuven: Peeters, 2000), pp. 120–9

Walicki, Andrzej, *A History of Russian Thought. From the Enlightenment to Marxism* (Oxford: Clarendon, 1988)

Ward, Benedicta, SLG (ed.), *The Prayers and Meditations of St Anselm with the 'Proslogion'* (London: Penguin, 1986 [1973])

Williams, Charles, *The Figure of Beatrice. A Study in Dante* (London: Faber and Faber, 1943)

—— *He Came Down from Heaven* (London: Heinemann, 1938)

—— *Outlines of Romantic Theology* (Berkeley, CA: Apocryphile Press, 2005)

—— *Religion and Love in Dante: the Theology of Romantic Love* (Westminster: Dacre Press, 1941)

Wozniuk, Vladimir (ed.), *Freedom, Faith and Dogma: Essays by V. S. Soloviev on Christianity and Judaism* (Albany, NY: State University of New York Press, 2008)
—— (ed.), *The Heart of Reality: Essays on Beauty, Love and Ethics by V. S. Soloviev* (Notre Dame, IN: University of Notre Dame Press, 2003)
—— (ed.), *Politics, Law, and Morality: Essays by V. S. Soloviev* (New Haven, CT: Yale University Press, 2000
Zatko, James K., *Descent into Darkness. The Destruction of the Roman Catholic Church in Russia, 1917–1923* (Notre Dame, IN: University of Notre Dame Press, 1965)
Zernov, Nicolas, *The Russian Religious Renaissance of the Twentieth Century* (London: Darton, Longman & Todd, 1963)
Zovko, Marie-Elise, *Natur und Gott. Das wirkungsgeschichtliche Verhältnis Schellings und Baaders* (Würzburg: Königshausen & Neumann, 1996)

www.ingramcontent.com/pod-product-compliance
Lightning Source LLC
Chambersburg PA
CBHW032258150426
43195CB00008BA/493